Sociological Evolution

Merging Morality and Economics

Vol. 1

T.M. Engel

Edited by Kris Williams

In loving memory of my Mom.

No child could have hoped or asked for better.

Dedicated to my wife, without whom this book never gets written. You are the definition of "my better half".
You have shown me how to be a better person and I am grateful for the life you have made possible for our family.

Table of Contents

Introduction

Open thy mouth, judge righteously,
and plead the cause of the poor
and needy.

Proverbs 31:9

The intent of this treatise is singular in that I hope to convince you of the necessity for us as a society to embrace a more spiritually fulfilling economic system. I believe economics and morality should be unified into a single endeavor, where the implications of both work more harmoniously to produce a system that properly sustains us spiritually as well as physically. Merging morality and economics is certainly not a new concept. Ancient Indian, Greek, Christian, Chinese, Islamic, and Japanese cultures, to name a few, all cultivated the belief that a society can only benefit from the ability to exercise restraint with respect to yearnings and the accumulation of wealth according to the moral standards reflected by their respective cultures. While open dialogue and debate is essential for any endeavor of this nature, we must begin by looking at what has been, not to criticize, but instead with appreciation for how far we have come and to determine the foundation for our next steps.

There are indeed clear indications that our society has the desire to find spiritual serenity. We already have a perception of what is wrong but making the leap to action is difficult. As a society, we are at the precipice but we're too scared to jump. Misconceptions and smokescreens employed by the richest one percent keep us too contented (or frightened) to attempt achieving the level of conviction needed to initiate this change. It's time for us to live up to the title we believe we deserve: "A Great Society." To do this though, we need to acknowledge that this title is not defined by GDP (Gross

Domestic Product), levels of technology, or the freedom to perform random charitable acts. Instead, it is determined by how equitably we all work to apply our productive abilities and technology to consistently ensure the welfare of all.

We already recognize many other areas of society that cannot function properly without clear consideration of their moral component. The Hippocratic Oath clearly establishes that the medical community must make decisions based not only on science and logic but also by thoroughly contemplating the ethical and moral implications of said decisions. Our own legal system leans heavily on verbal oaths sworn to God in a court of law which lend validity to the speaker's words as truth. This same system often determines guilt or innocence predicated on evidence that establishes a person's state of mind. For example, the difference between first and second degree murder is a judgement based upon not just physical and verifiable proof but of assertions pertaining to the mental state and intent of a person. Isn't a hate-crime charge the very definition of presuming a person's intent beyond their physical actions alone?

There has been a concerted effort to ignore the moral and ethical implications of economics but we can no longer deny that these ramifications apply here as well. We must open our eyes to the harrowing truth that capitalism is designed to provoke conflict amongst the 99 percent of society so that we pitilessly fight each other for a greater share of a single sliver of the overall wealth of our society. This intentional misdirection provides the one percent free rein to gorge upon the majority of that wealth.

This book is not about the currently proposed pseudo-socialist capitalist ideals of the liberal left politicos, nor do I support such ideals. Both the right wing and left wing politicians currently stand united as members of the one percent or, at best, act as sycophants for them. I do not suggest a chaotic free-for-all where no one is held accountable for anything or taking from the workers to give to the poor like some demented Robin Hood, as it is now. This is neither an ignorant declaration to promote giving goods to the lazy for free nor a proposal to take what is earned away from those who have justly earned it.

Life is not fair. I understand that. If it were fair, people would not be suffering and dying in the first place. Evil exists here on Earth and we are not capable of changing that fact. This is not some fanciful tale of imagination where every child gets a pony, no one ever gets sick or dies, and we all live happily ever after. Such ideas are foolish and a waste of everyone's time. It is important to understand that perfection is never the proposed alternative. The point is that we have each been granted the gift of free will by God and what we *choose* to do with that free will while here on Earth *will* have a ripple effect on the lives of those around us. This, our ability to exercise our free will for the good of others, to make a difference, is what sets us apart from the plants and the animals. We cannot save everyone but, sadly, we aren't even saving those that could be - and herein lies the heart of the problem.

I do not propose world-wide disarmament with idealistic and improbable dreams of world peace and harmony. This isn't a dissertation about opening our borders to everyone without consideration of their willingness to legally participate in whatever economic system we might have in place. While these circumstances would be wonderful to see, it is not pragmatic to expose ourselves to possible exploitation or to very real security risks. While I represent no particular affiliation and do not intend to preach, I feel compelled to express my personal beliefs and understanding of what I comprehend my religious obligations to be. At the same time, I feel it is not necessary that others hold the same religious beliefs that I do in order to understand the moral depravity that capitalism supports. Although I do refer to the teachings of Jesus to find support, most religions and spiritual teachings worldwide support these same ideals. So, despite religious differences, I believe we can all find common ground in Altruistically Inspired Societal Economics.

AISE

*Like slavery and apartheid, poverty
is not natural. It is man-made and
it can be overcome and eradicated
by the actions of human beings.
And overcoming poverty is not a
gesture of charity. It is an act of
justice. It is the protection of a
fundamental human right, the
right to dignity and a decent life.
While poverty persists, there is no
true freedom...
Sometimes it falls on a generation
to be great. You can be that great
generation. Let your greatness
blossom.*

Nelson Mandela

Altruistically Inspired Societal Economics (AISE) is an
economic system designed to bring about the true reallocation
of wealth. The term is original so as not to conjure
preconceived, visceral reactions or misconceptions at its
utterance, as is the case with so many conventional economic
expressions. While the term is admittedly a bit lengthy, it is
intended to be as accurately descriptive as possible.
"Altruistically" ensures that the moral aspect cannot be ignored
or displaced. "Inspired" reminds us that as altruistic as the
intention is, there will be times when difficult choices must be
made. At those times we must not abandon the greater good
for unavoidable minor issues. "Societal" makes it clear that we
are in fact a society and therefore, by definition,
interdependent upon each other. A fact that we often

consciously try to ignore. "Economics", because it is in fact a systematic methodology for equitably distributing goods and services.

AISE is not about coddling the lazy but instead relies heavily on individual liability. The success of this system would depend upon a higher level of accountability from each member of the society than we have in the current pseudo-socialist capitalistic system. AISE is about putting the value of innocent human life above that of profit realization or the accumulation of trinkets. It puts more emphasis on providing a meaningful life for those with disabilities based on our actual capability rather than on spending only what we can "afford" before some random budget is depleted. It applies more value to actually curing people with cancer than cashing in on the fame and financial dividends of that ultimate lottery ticket: "the cure." It seeks to provide a safe and stable home for every foster child in this country, not just handing over pocket change as a solution while lamenting the failures of our system. Instead of the individual being responsible solely for his/her own financial security, the individual becomes responsible for performing his/her equitable share of labor. In return, all of the individual's needs and desires are equitably addressed.

People could mistakenly believe we will have less in an altruistic society like AISE, as theatrical propagandist images abound of work-weary, slovenly dressed, broken people who labor deep into the night. I find this mistaken imagery quite ironic since it accurately represents the state of industrial workers in this very country in the early twentieth century. Capitalism is responsible for producing the exact image that we currently fear a system such as AISE would produce. The reality is that the only people who have less in an AISE society are those who are currently millionaires and billionaires. EVERYONE else will have more. They may not have everything they want and possibly still not everything they need but they will *all* have more than they currently do. Considering the average net worth for a member of the top one percent is roughly $8.4 million, while the net worth for the median American family is

$120,000, how could one logically believe they would be worse off if this wealth were equitably redistributed? There is a 69% difference between the averages of the top one percent versus the 99 percent. Politicians and celebrities (rich people) like to talk about the reallocation of wealth but it usually entails reallocating *your* wealth to other people. After all the speeches and proposals are made, the well-to-do still stand with seven figure bank accounts and diverse real estate holdings, each worth more than the combined value of everyone in your neighborhood. It is crucial to remember the only people who do not gain in AISE are the members of the one percent. Because of these facts, it is important to consider the source before you consider the criticism of an altruistic economic system.

We currently produce to maximum efficiency of the given resources, which is supported by the very doctrine of the free market economist. This success in production however, is achieved with minimal compensation to the laborer as is dictated by our need to sustain ourselves and the tolerance by the one percent of this need. In an AISE society, we are able to maintain the same level of efficient production, but are not limited by the amount of compensation for mere subsistence. We are then free to consume all the fruits produced by the labor of the masses. We would actually have the ability to consume more, labor less, or a combination of both. This is because our labor would no longer need to create a surplus to be designated as "profit" for the benefit of the one percent. In this way, everything that we produce would be shared amongst all of us. Currently, we labor and receive a fraction of the fruits of that effort. This is why we see such affluence on one extreme end of the scale and shortages to everyone else.

If you put in the work to earn $200 but have to give $40 to someone who does nothing but observe you working, you would think that unfair. Perhaps you would even think it extremely unfair. This is why many people have such distaste for "social programs." Yet, that is essentially the same as what occurs today when you perform the labor and corporate leaders profit from your labors. If you are being paid $200, what you produce in that time frame is certainly worth significantly more than that to those who are profiting from your labor. Certainly you are not the only cog in the process and there are many other costs to consider but, even taking that all into account, the product you produce has value in excess of what you are compensated. That is the end result of capitalism. Is the CEO, sitting in his or her Crystal Palace manipulating numbers, really that much more worthy of skimming the fruits of your labors than the recipient of a "social program?"

The primary justification for corporate profit or business ownership is that those at the top assume all the risk. I've used this justification too. What do they risk? Money. We've been convinced to believe in the legitimacy and importance of trickledown economics and investment risk to justify large capital-owning corporations taking large percentages from what we have produced. Because of this economic system, they are allowed to tax us and make a profit from our labors, but it is wrong to consider the welfare of other workers? I'm not talking about accepting high taxation from the one percent so they can hand out the money to whomever they deem worthy with their futile social programs. I'm talking about eliminating the one percent altogether so no one is profiting from the labors of the workers except the workers. In this scenario, no one would control an obscene amount of power and wealth and all the workers equitably share in the fruits of their combined efforts.

> *O believers, be you securers of justice, witnesses for God. Let not detestation for a people move you not to be equitable; be equitable -- that is nearer to god-fearing. And fear God; surely God is aware of the things you do.*

The Qur' ān (5:8)

The above quote is one of several translations from a passage in the Qur' ān. Other versions use the word "just" instead of "equitable." This quote is another example of the way different cultures apply moral values to their economic realities and also serves to substantiate my assertion that many world religions view the subject of equitability in a similar light. And although I use the term equitable often, it is not a cheap trick to avoid specificity but simply a matter of reality. When everyone puts forth their best effort for the support of the community, all share equitably in the goods and services produced by that effort. Equitable, however, does not mean equal. A two month-old infant does not need the same type or amount of rations as a 200 lb. athletic male. To insist that both get equal shares would be illogical and wasteful. Equitable is already a widely recognized legal term applied throughout our society. Beyond that, just about every relationship on Earth relies on people consenting to what they both agree to be equitable terms. Otherwise, we would be exchanging one egg for one shoe or ten pounds of liver for ten pounds of bricks.

We need to be cautious in making declarations of being fair. What is fair? As an example, if I were to ask my children who cooked breakfast this morning, they would say I did. Who cleaned up after breakfast? I did. Who bought the groceries to make breakfast? Again, that was me. Who earned the money to buy those groceries? Once again, that was my responsibility. So they ate breakfast but yet I'm the one who did everything that was necessary to make breakfast possible. Is that fair? Well, life would be pretty hard if we only lived by what was fair.

As a Christian, I believe we are all sinners and therefore unworthy to enter the Kingdom of Heaven on our own attributes. It is only through the suffering and sacrifice of Jesus Christ that we can do so. He earned salvation for us and yet we are and continue to be sinners. Is that fair? Absolutely not. As a Christian, one should never be concerned with "being fair" but only with the right thing to do. After all, isn't that what Jesus continually taught in the New Testament? If someone strikes you, do not seek retribution but instead offer the other cheek? If someone sues you for your outer garment, give them also your undergarment. The Good Samaritan did not concern himself with how much time and money it would cost to help the beaten man. If he had acted only after considering the fairness of offering his assistance, he most likely would not have done so. The beaten man had been robbed and likely would not have been able to compensate the Samaritan for his costs or time. And at that time, Samaritans were looked down upon and, therefore, there was no guarantee the Samaritan would have been viewed in a better light for performing this good deed. In all probability, excuses would have been made for his unexpected charity and he would not have gained any favor for his good work. Not very fair indeed.

In truth, are we ever really appropriately compensated for our deeds, time, or effort? Isn't that why, in the rare instances of honest compensation, we tend to make grandiose proclamations about how fulfilling such an experience was? The majority of people do not enjoy that type of fulfillment on a day to day basis. At this point, I'm just discussing the probability of satisfaction with purchases in general, such as gas, groceries, car insurance, dental work, etc. I'm not even referring to shopper's remorse and the common dissatisfaction that material procurement can lead to. Honestly, how often do you feel truly well compensated and therapeutically fulfilled after a financial transaction? Do you ever really feel like you have more than enough? Are you able to eat how you want to eat, go where you want to go? So for all the freedom and choice and free market advantages, are you really as satisfied as the propaganda says you should be? Do you actually have the socio-economic mobility that has been the cornerstone of the draw to this country since its inception? Do you actually own everything that you possess or are you indebted and beholden to so many faceless, nameless money managers that you have no idea what is actually yours?

Don't be fooled either if you are lucky enough to "own" your house. If you can't pay or are unwilling to pay the property taxes for that house, every year, it will not belong to you for long. That concept has been a difficult one for me to grasp. It appalls me that the one percent have successfully managed to irrevocably dig their claws into the one item of the greatest monetary value that most Americans will ever possess. That house will never truly belong to you or to your heirs unless you and they are able to continually pay the one percent for the privilege of possessing it. So much for private "ownership". While eminent domain certainly is not a common occurrence, it is legal and is in fact carried out. Certain jurisdictions, not HOAs but jurisdictions, maintain the right to fine home owners for violating random property codes. Failure to comply with these codes can result in liens being applied to the house. It is also legal for local jurisdictions to condemn a house that fails to meet code regulations.

So let's say there is someone who has a house that is old and in need of repairs but is currently living paycheck to paycheck. These homeowners pay taxes to the same government entity that can condemn their house, evict them, and leave them homeless. How does this make sense? If you are poor and not able to maintain your house to the standard specified by law, the solution is to evict you from your home? Normally the motivating factor behind such policies is not public safety but rather the desire to remove structures that are lowering neighboring property values. These things happen often enough to know they are real and that the government can, in essence, punish you for being poor. This is the truth, right now, under the vaunted protection and freedom of capitalism upheld by a democratic republic.

This is not about humanism or humanitarianism per se, since the definitions of both of these concepts openly deny the importance of divinity. Yes, I argue in this work for the need to make humanitarian concern the focal point of our decision making process. But I do so because I disagree with the focal point currently revolving around making a profit. I do not think it is right to deny the existence of God or His importance and I am strongly motivated by the belief that it is in fact His will for us to disregard profits and to start caring for each other as fellow humans. I'm walking a tight rope here because on the one hand I am openly religious and make no apologies for it.

Quite the opposite, my religion teaches that I am obligated to go forth and evangelize. Honestly satisfying this charge is part of my motivation for bringing this work to light. If I can help to strengthen one person's beliefs or bring another person to God, then that would be quite satisfying. At the same time, I do not believe that humanitarian concern is the sole proprietorship, or even the sole responsibility, of Christians. If I fail at bringing any one person closer to God, I hope then to at least convince others of the moral depravity of capitalism and the humanitarian benefit of an AISE society. I will not apologize for or disguise my beliefs, but instead I will simultaneously state my beliefs and respectfully attempt to reach out to as many as I can with my economic ideas.

Altruistically Inspired Societal Economics is not about getting things for free. This is the mistake made by the current pseudo-socialist capitalist liberal democratic movement. They may appear to be the same, but there are critical differences. It is maddening how the latter attempts to pass itself off as similar in structure to AISE and I believe this is not wholly unintentional. One difference between the two is that where AISE provides for social services that are truly universal, pseudo-socialist capitalism prevents those who finance the greatest portion of these programs from benefitting because they, ironically, make too much to qualify as a recipient. The other critical difference is that AISE can reasonably answer how to provide for these universal services. The dialogue begins by openly admitting we need to redefine the cost of goods and services, both in the procurement and distribution end of the process. Pseudo-socialist capitalism somehow magically believes that everything can be paid for while still applying the current understanding of cost. Of course the only way this is plausible is by way of massive taxation, which is what Canada and the more socialist nations of Europe have done. But admitting that in America would be political suicide so it is deemed better to use creative and vague language to answer this pertinent question. There are already lines of people filling out paperwork so they can return home and wait for money to be sent to them, as well as large numbers of people panhandling on the streets, so it is illogical for this to be proposed as a possible negative effect of AISE. The purpose is not to support such a broken system further but instead to work toward eliminating it altogether. With AISE, everyone would be gainfully employed in whatever function they are able and there would be no need for panhandling, charity, or "social programs".

Life for humans, for the majority of history, has been based on a fear of shortages. Economics in ancient times was applied with the main purpose of addressing in advance, the issue of shortages that were certain to occur so that order could be maintained. So the application of an economic system that feeds on that same kind of fear and imbues a desire to hoard does make some sense. Shortages applied to every aspect of human life including, but not limited to, the vital elements of water, food, and later medicine. Yet many researchers agree that economics was not merely an exercise in the allocation of goods but was an attempt to adhere to moral standards while doing so. Certainly this must be taken in context for the moral standards acceptable for the time and culture in question. It was a universally held "fact" that societies needed to have a hierarchical system in order to maintain order. This misplaced belief naturally affected every other social system and is why some of their practices and beliefs seem to conflict with each other. While we could sit and ridicule the existence of racism, bias, slavery, sexism, and intolerance to diversity in what previous societies found to be moral, do we really stand with unblemished hands? Are we the founders of the new "Universally Accepted Land" or do we too potentially stand to be as critically judged in the future as we criticize those before us?

We have made tremendous social advancement. To deny this fact is ignorance and unwarranted negativity bordering on the misanthropic. We have our problems, but this country does represent the most profound level of impartial diversity in history and should receive due recognition as such.

That being said, previous cultures that were less accepting still incorporated their moral fabric into their economic functions. Whereas we stand haughty and self-righteous, we utterly obliterate morality from our economic function. Succeed or die, that defines capitalism. In the meat factories of the early twentieth century, if you cut off a finger you had better keep working or you would be fired. There were no accommodations for those with impairments, congenital or work related. That is the spirit and application of true capitalism.

The situation has changed in more ways than one though. Not only have we progressed in the acceptance of allowing more diverse people equal opportunity at gaining their own wealth, we also do not face shortages like previous generations. Ironically, we create our own shortages now. It is no longer simply a lack of availability of clean water but the cost associated with it that creates shortages. Medicine can be mass produced to suit whatever needs are established but again it is cost that dictates and creates shortages. As I will discuss at length later, food is another shortage that we create. We have eliminated polio and we can sustain the lives of those with AIDS indefinitely now. We have the means to avoid suffering the consequences of shortages yet we curiously choose to allow the suffering regardless. The ironic part is that we sit here and defend this choice and cling to capitalism while the rich sigh and laugh. We help them to maintain their position in society and they are content to do so as they know few, if any, shortages. They need not suffer these same consequences as they possess the means to make sure difficulties disappear for themselves.

What if a family member got sick suddenly or the car died tomorrow morning? Would you have enough to comfortably see it through, or would your life and lifestyle be utterly thrown out of balance? Sure even in an Altruistically Inspired Societal Economy there would be the fear of sickness, accidental death, and famine. So AISE isn't Shangri Lai and I am not implying that it is. But the difference is that these fears are possible in both capitalism and AISE. What differs is that in AISE, you do not need to worry about going hungry...while standing in front of a store filled with food. If you have not planned properly or if circumstances go badly for you, though that is exactly what happens in capitalism. In AISE, you do not need to worry about dying because you could not afford to buy a specific mass produced medication due to a lack of funds or insurance.

So why not work together to eliminate some of these risks and fears, rather than working separately? Of course if you are in the one percent, you can have both security and unfettered luxury already. Famine and disease of course remain concerns but by pooling resources and eliminating monetary concerns, the society as a whole will be healthier, more satisfied, and more productive. Doesn't everyone want to get paid more because they fear running out of money? I don't see Warren Buffet or Donald Trump offering massive discounts on anything they sell just because they "have enough." Isn't a lot of that fear based on what would happen if something bad occurred? So many people who have wealth choose to hoard money due to a fear of deprivation during hard times. Others choose to live in the moment for fear that if they don't, they will live in misery their whole life, constantly waiting for the bad moment to come. Their philosophy then becomes: why save for a possible problem? It is easier to believe it is best to live life to the fullest right now. I propose that we instead work in unison to eliminate many of these risks and fears altogether.

Misconceptions of Socialism

*It is the mark of an educated mind
to be able to entertain a thought
without accepting it.*

Aristotle

The terms *communism* and *socialism* have been so misused by now that they are unrecognizable from their original definitions. While this is in part due to the ignorance of society, it is not unintentional. Socialism was generically considered a more refined and restrained movement, whereas communism was an unapologetic call for blood and revolution. Remember that this was a call for a revolution by the people against the oppressive state, which is a reality that is utterly opposed to the common American vision of communism. We normally envision communism as the state snatching control away from the people, and so characterized as tyrannical. Other than the more revolutionary and aggressive approach of the communists, both socialists and communists believed in the same outcome. Both approaches were declarations by the working class that they refused to allow the one percent to exploit them any longer. For both economic theories, it was the goal that the fruits of everyone's labor be shared equitably. Is it any wonder then that those in power and control of money, everywhere, would willingly unite, using propaganda and deceit to dissuade others from joining this revolution?

These members of the one percent have promoted the misuse of these terms in order to create a Pavlovian response to the words *communism* and *socialism*. What is the first thing that comes to mind when you hear those words? For me, it is still the "red hoard of the Godless commie Soviets," because that was the phrase most often repeated throughout my formative years. For others, the conditioning may be linked to the Chinese, Vietnamese, Cubans, or North Koreans. And yet, none of those countries are examples of communism. We were taught to hate the "commies" because they were wanton defilers of freedom and democracy. This concept has become so strongly ingrained in us as a society that simply hearing the term causes an visceral reaction. The propaganda campaign has been hugely successful. It has taken me over thirty years to see through this programming and for many, it is so effectively entrenched that if one were to challenge these ideas, it likely would result in a backlash of anger and accusations questioning their patriotism. This, in essence, is brainwashing intended to provoke such a strong reaction that one would refuse to intellectually consider any differing opinion. This knee-jerk response is the desired result of the vilification of socialism by those promoting capitalism.

One of the greatest misconceptions about communism is that it was intended, and is necessary, to exist as a dictatorship. One of the last lines of the *Communist Manifesto* claims that it is the desire of communists for the:

> *...agreement and unification of democratic parties around the world.*

That's right; communism was intended to exist in conjunction with democracy, not in opposition to it as we have been mistakenly led to believe. The Soviet Union and China are prime examples of oppressive oligarchies (where small factions seize control of a country). This type of political control usually emerges through use of fear tactics, manipulation, and oppression. This is not communism. North Korea and Cuba are examples of dictatorships, not communism. People have asked me why these countries are referred to as communist if they are not. My response is merely: if I change my first name to "Doctor," would I then, indeed be a doctor? Simply changing my name to Doctor doesn't actually make me one, just as adding the word "City" to the name of a specific locale does not immediately set it on equal par with New York City. Further examples of my point are illustrated by the names of the countries technically known as The Union of Soviet Socialist Republics, The People's Republic of China, and The Socialist Republic of Vietnam respectively. Devolving into a battle of semantics here would be futile, seeing as how none of the above actually refer to themselves as communists in their own official titles.

To continue, the United States is a republic founded upon the same structure as the Roman Empire. A republic is defined as a country whose representatives are democratically elected to represent the interests of those who elected them. Is there really a valid argument to categorize the countries above as republics at the time they adopted their country names? The Democratic People's Republic of Korea (that's *North* Korea by the way) tops the improbability list in that department and I would challenge anyone to prove the veracity of a claim for their being a democracy or a republic, based solely on the official title of the country. The founders of these governments hid behind the titles of communist and socialist in order to pacify and deceive the public while they usurped authority and seized power.

Current liberals in this country might wish to consider the above fact as they become enamored by the enticing rhetoric of politicians who wish to implement pseudo-socialist capitalist controls of their own. That may sound contrary to my position at this point but I will clarify that later. The wealthy one percent of other countries were more than happy to support labeling these oppressive oligarchies and dictatorships as communist, in order to substantiate their need to vilify the ideal. The heinous acts performed by these repressive leaders made hating communism very easy indeed. The problem is that this hatred of communism was based on the actions of corrupt leaders of oligarchies and dictatorships. That is as logical as deciding to hate all vegetables because a certified organic farmer deceitfully used chemicals. Hating vegetables due to the dishonest actions of one person makes no sense. Just don't buy from the deceitful farmer any longer and get your vegetables from an honest source. But the one percent wants you to instinctively hate communism regardless of the facts or logic of the argument.

It is quite often assumed by critics that a communal economy has not been embraced because it does not work. That does make sense. If it is such a great system, then why hasn't a society yet implemented it? This is a logical, if not misconstrued, question but isn't a more obvious reason for this the fact that those in power (i.e. those with the most to lose with the successful implementation of AISE) have manipulated perceptions to make it seem undesirable? Why would any wealthy person support Altruistically Inspired Societal Economics? Why would anyone in a position of power, and therefore a beneficiary of the influential wealthy, support Altruistically Inspired Societal Economics? If the 99 percent continue to bicker and take from each other, doesn't that just secure the luxury of the one percent? Doesn't it make sense that the wealthy want the idea of AISE to be so instinctively disgusting to us that it prevents any intelligent discussion of the real and pertinent facts? Why is such focus put on the friction between the middle income segment and those in poverty when the difference between these two groups is razor thin? The liberal one percent creates friction by taking from the middle income segment to create a state-dependent welfare segment. The conservative one percent creates friction by convincing the middle income segment to hate the "lazy, unmotivated" welfare segment just created. We need to stop letting the one percent manipulate us against each other. The one percent is creating the animosity among us that makes altruistic economics seem so impossible.

The closest example of successful AISE implementation is observable in the Native American societies. Native American cultures did not believe in widespread private ownership but rather, in communal ownership. No one person owned the land

and, as a tribe, everyone was responsible for the welfare of everyone else. Granted, it was not a perfect system but many of the problems present in modern-day capitalism were not an issue in Native American economics. To be clear, I'm specifically referring to the economic system and not the government or religion. Just because this is the best functioning example drawn from history, it does not mean that in order to follow a similar economic system one would need to duplicate the structure of any one given Native American tribe. The communal economy of the Native Americans was not the cause of their fall to U.S. expansion. To believe so would be narrow minded and fails to consider a plethora of other relevant factors. For instance, their technological disadvantage is as easily linked to cultural, religious, and social factors as it is to choices of economic function. Suffice it to say, their effective communal economy is simply an example of the positive effects that AISE can have in a society.

I have heard about the recent pledge by the ultra-wealthy to donate massive portions of "their" wealth. But unlike many others, I am not one to offer praise for a promise. Instead, I believe in reserving praise for those who actually act on or fulfill said promises. Would you rather the promise of food or to actually be fed? The latter act will fill your stomach but the former, not so much. I have yet to see a billionaire give up any substantial portion of their fortune. I believe this campaign is yet another empty promise to trick the masses into believing the filthy rich are actually benevolent and charitable.

The issue is not whether AISE is more beneficial for humankind, but in how to overcome the concentrated confusion and deception of those in power to sabotage the idea of it. In an altruistic economy those with the most to lose are those who are already in power, because they control the most influence and a staggering proportion of the wealth. Why would they want that influence and wealth evenly distributed amongst the people? Remember that these people do not work anyway and they are completely secure in financial terms. One can certainly argue that, in spite of their financial wealth, health is not a guarantee. It is true that being rich does not guarantee health. But if you were to develop a debilitating disease tomorrow, could you afford to hire five assistants, buy a specially modified vehicle, assume the new $1000/month medication expense, and lose your income? These people can and that's the difference. How much stress and burden would you and your loved ones be under trying to pay for and accommodate your new needs in the same situation? This is just another example of the kind of security that their wealth provides them. So it is logical that they would do everything to keep it.

How much do you hate the idea of a tax increase? That's only a small portion of your wealth being redistributed. You likely have limited amounts of power and influence, which is not even in the same solar system as the kind of power these people wield. But if we, the 99 percent, banded together and demanded an equitable dispersion of wealth, the one percent would have to face losing the ability to do anything they want, whenever they want. Doesn't it make sense that they would avoid such a fall with every fiber of their being? Let's not forget that the higher taxes causing you frustration are likely created by the pseudo-socialist capitalist system that is currently in place. That means you will be working just as hard for less, so that others who do not work can prosper. Can you imagine how much more strenuously those in power would oppose AISE than you would a tax increase? They would, and do, throw their full weight into manipulating the facts and obscuring the truth in order to convince society that Altruistically Inspired Societal Economics is detrimental and that capitalism is the most beneficial, nay the only way, for the working segment to achieve happiness. This is why true altruistic economics has so rarely been seen.

Paradoxically, as phobic as we are to real socialism, we in fact have socialist programs throughout our system. Ironically, we staunchly defend a system that has numerous socialist programs and restrictions to free market economics but since we slap a **CAPITALIST** bumper sticker on it, it's all good. This is as ridiculous as putting an **ORGANIC** sticker on a can of Cheese Whiz. Isn't it a good thing that corporations can no longer pit the workers against each other in a bidding war to see who will work for the least amount of money? That protective mechanism is called the minimum wage and is not a capitalist concept. Aren't labor safety regulations good? That's not a capitalist concept either. Aren't child labor laws good? That is entirely a communist ideal written about in the *Communist Manifesto*. Regulation of any kind is theoretically not supportive of the free market economy. Yet every time we de-regulate an industry in order to stimulate the free market system it fails, epically. The ludicrous belief is that such action will benefit everyone, as the particular industry will then flourish due to unrestricted growth.

This repetitive failure does not hinder us from continuing to repeat the same idiocy though. Deregulation of the stock market- fail. Deregulation of mortgage management- fail. Airline Deregulation Act of 1978- fail. The 1999 Financial Services Modernization Act repealed the Glass-Steagall Act of 1933 which barred the common ownership of banks, insurance companies, and securities firms. This resulted in the freedom these companies needed to merge and begin to create convoluted and interrelated investment vehicles. This directly contributed not only to the occurrence of the 2008 crash but to the severity of it as well. This is because, instead of being able to compartmentalize damage, as was intended by the Glass-Steagall Act of 1933, it became all encompassing. So we can see how wildly successful that deregulation effort turned out to be.

Each and every one of these ill-conceived deregulation movements resulted in a fiasco that harmed the public. Let's be honest, the genesis of these movements originated from the self-serving desires of the business owners, the lobbyists they empowered, and the corrupt politicians that authorized them. It is the general public that had to suffer the eventual consequences each time. Not once did the promised benefits of competitive pricing and more efficient delivery of goods and services come to fruition. This is because laissez faire (hands off) capitalism does not work unless you have wealth. It is absolutely no better than the medieval economic systems of old, defined by the oppressive and exploitive control by the one percent. Marx and Engels correctly predicted that the exploitation of the proletariat (workers) by the one percent would eventually become so oppressive that the workers would revolt. They were absolutely correct in their estimation of capitalism and it is only through the application of increasingly strict regulation and the socialization of capitalism that it has survived.

Now some might say that is not true. Capitalism has provided excellent programs like public schooling for everyone, PBS, the American Red Cross, and disability benefits. Yes, but these are all socialized programs and charities. These programs do not fall into the scope of capitalism and so cannot logically be employed as a counter argument in this scenario. Most Americans are quick to defend and openly recognize these as positive organizations, greatly deserving of continued support, yet these organizations represent the antithesis of capitalism. Our hearts apparently know better than our brains. While we applaud the great benefits of capitalism, which are in fact socialism, we absurdly lament the effects of those failed policies which originate from pure capitalistic ideals.

Socialism was intended to be the liberation of the workers from the oppression of the one percent. Marx and Engels correctly identify capitalism as nothing more than a systematic way for the one percent to exploit the working segment. They correctly assert that capitalism strips all value from human life except for its monetary worth. It does not matter that you are a human being that is suffering and needs medicine; if you do not have enough money to pay for it, you cannot have it. How is this not the very definition of ignoring your worth as a human and placing value on your life or wellbeing? In this case the worth of your wellbeing could be as little as $7.97 for a bottle of cold medicine or perhaps a few hundred dollars for antibiotics. We are so accepting of our economic system that we rarely, if ever, think in these simple but real terms. We have become conditioned to recognize the $7.97 as nothing more than a simple accumulation of costs and profit margins for a product. We no longer see that in reality it also represents the value we believe easing your suffering is worth.

Quality of work is also given a new value system based on monetary worth in capitalism. The craftsmanship and quality of products must constantly be weighed against profitability. If too much quality is put into the product it necessitates a higher price be charged, thereby making it too costly for the general public to afford. High quality craftsmanship typically comes with an inflated price. In AISE, if the same natural resources were required to produce the same chair as in capitalism, what reason would there be to not produce the best chair possible? The answer is none. But in capitalism, it is vital for the fastest process to be used with the expectation that there will be a number of defects. The key to profitability is to make sure the defects are not critical in nature and do not occur at a rate that would be detrimental to profitability.

In AISE, one asks why a laborer who can make fifty baseball bats a day that can be sold to a store for $20 each only gets paid $1 per bat? Now a good capitalist will explain that there are many separate costs associated with production and they must all be accounted for in the overall price. It would further be pointed out that since the factory owner is the owner of the capital necessary for production, he or she is deserving of profit as compensation for assuming the initial financial risk. Altruistically Inspired Societal Economics asks, why can't everyone who puts forth the effort and hard work share equally in the fruits of that effort and labor? What's more, exactly what gives the "owner of capital" the right to this prestigious distinction? Are we to just accept this concept as if it were awarded as a birth right?

It is time to do away with these antiquated beliefs. Just as with the slave owners, to make things right there needs to be drastic change. Does anyone truly believe our country owes the former slave owners an apology or monetary compensation for the act of freeing their slaves? After all, those slaves were their lawful property before that law was changed. Was it wrong to take "property" from the slave owners in order to make a better world and rectify an unjust practice? If you agree with me that it was not unjust, can you also recognize that reallocating the 34% of national investment wealth and 28% of the national property value that is "owned" by the one percent to the other 318 million Americans is not at all dissimilar? Which is worse: taking that wealth away, or allowing such a disproportionate sham to occur in the first place? Should we instead defend the rights of a few thousand while disregarding the suffering of millions?

This is not a proposal for blood, revolution, or anarchy. It's not even about hating the one percent. I'd like to think that I would have the same feeling about all this even if I had been born into a family with money to burn, but certainly I cannot guarantee that. So, I can look upon these people with indignant, self-righteous disdain but what is that going to accomplish? Better to acknowledge that I could be them if circumstances had been different and to simply continue on with what I at least believe to be morally correct, right now. The actions taken in the Reformation Period, ending Apartheid, the American Revolution, the Indian Independence Movement, and the Civil Rights Movement all serve as precedent for this idea. In all of these situations "property" was redistributed and laws were changed to correct a moral wrong. So such things have occurred before, why can't they happen again? If we argue that capitalism *must* be maintained for fear of "stealing" from the one percent, then we have truly lost our way. Forget that it is a system designed to gain and maintain this perverted amount of wealth for them in the first place.

When the preservation of an institution (even a noble one, which capitalism is not) becomes more important than the welfare of those it is supposed to safeguard, it is time to dissolve the institution. Would you tell a battered wife she is obligated to continue abiding by the marital vows since she willingly entered into the marriage contract in the first place? Why then should we be obligated to recognize "ownership" by the one percent, an illusion that only exists because of a system originally designed by them to abuse us? Lastly, isn't the alleged greatest attribute of our system the fact that *"We the People"* have the power to legally implement change as we see fit, based on the cultural needs of the time? I think they call them Amendments...or something. Many of those Amendments had profound impact on the future course of this nation and largely in a very positive manner.

A Condensed History

Facts do not cease to exist because they are ignored.

Aldous Huxley

Originally leadership was based on brute force. The most physically dominant person was the leader or, the Alpha. Most people are aware of this concept due to its prevalence in the animal kingdom. In the early stages of human evolution, we selected leaders based on these same traits. Humans then evolved intellectually and, although it may not have been on a conscious level, began to realize the intrinsic value of a leader who was more than just big and strong. This was the person who not only figured out how to produce and maintain fire but had also realized that to withhold it unless given authority and status was to his advantage. This began the next stage of leadership development which continues to this day: the practice of leadership through manipulation and control. Of course the current leaders wanted their offspring and surviving heirs to inherit the same luxury and influence they enjoyed. So what better way to cement their position than by combining the right of leadership with religious superstition? By creating the belief of divine right to leadership, the leaders of early civilizations cunningly ensured their lineage for many generations and established a common human practice that would endure for thousands of years. Many of them probably believed the divine right theory was real but the fact remains that they chose a self-serving belief to ensure their status.

This practice developed into clearly delineated social classes based on assumed natural orders of superiority. We have evolved past this but only to an extent. In the not so distant past, status classifications were determined by assumptions of genetics. At that time, the comprehension of genetics did not exist as it does today but was instead encapsulated within a broader category: nature. And so it was determined that one collective of people, a nation, or a race was superior to another because of their birthright or because the gods favored one group over the others. You were who you were born to be and that was it. A warrior was born a warrior; a jester was born a jester, and so on. While we have advanced beyond this, in no small part due to the spread of Christianity, we still suffer the same prejudices to an extent. Christianity helped foster the belief that one could rise above one's station and that it was possible to ignore racial and national lines of distinction. This provides one valid reason why there was a concerted effort to stamp it out. After all, such ideas are dangerous. Within Christianity, no matter what the station of one's birth, salvation was offered equally to everyone. Heaven was a place where titles would hold no meaning among humans. Many other religions of the time period taught that the entitlements and advantages of this life would carry on into the next, so this new concept was somewhat radical. A dirty beggar now had the same opportunity to gain salvation in Christ and sit as equals with an Earthly king in Heaven. While this was treacherous thinking, it was restricted to the afterlife and the divine right theory was still ubiquitously employed to keep order here on Earth.

So, for most of humanity, we see the development of hereditary control of wealth and power. Monarchies or straight dictatorships were the predominant form of control over the masses. However, this control could not be maintained singularly. Practically every culture developed a bourgeoisie class, a sub segment which was given greater status and wealth than the masses in return for helping the monarchies maintain their control. Think of it as high level management, if you will. Previous generations of the bourgeoisie were content to suffer the abuses of royalty or tribal chiefs. This, in part, was because they had no choice and greatly feared for what they had to lose.

No matter the insults or abuses they may have experienced, it was still better to be bourgeoisie than to be stripped of what privileges and wealth they had and be cast down to join the peasants. This is the same paralysis that the conventional middle income segment of this country faces. This is neither irony nor coincidence but by the design of the one percent in this country who control well over half the wealth. We complain about rising taxes, blatant malfeasance by politicians, and inequitable pseudo-socialist capitalist practices, but because we fear losing what we have, we continue on like the bourgeoisie of old. It's not exactly the same but the similarity lies in the fact that fear of loss is an effective paralytic.

The existence of royalty and tribal chiefs established order and was the accepted way of keeping the peasants in their place. Who would be foolish enough to follow another peasant in a revolt against the deity-chosen leaders? Such a thought was not only foolish but blasphemous. Then, something happened in Europe. Royalty and religion became engaged in a very public and prolonged disagreement. English history is rife with multiple claimants in conflict over the throne but there was always an established validity to these claims by way of hereditary terms. This new conflict that had erupted in Europe centered on actual schisms within the Catholic Church, thereby questioning the validity of the establishment itself. The creation of the Church of England, the Holy Roman Empire, and the Protestant Reformation all served to weaken the people's sense of reverence and awe of, as well as their dependence on, royalty who could confirm their claims of birthright to the throne. While in hindsight it is clear to us how flawed such a thought process was, it took some time for this realization to occur. This progression of thought continued until a time when the bourgeoisie saw an opportunity to exploit the fact that the masses were less than enthralled with royalty and were, in fact, beginning to openly reject the notion of selection by God for royals to rule over others.

The bourgeoisie became emboldened and began to usurp more and more control. In Japan, we see a similar development, but with different circumstances. After years of civil war, Minamoto Yoritomo assumed the mantle of Shogun and, by doing so, was able to assume considerable control over the country. The emperor still commanded respect and was beyond reproach, the Bakufu continued to have influence, but the Shogun became the de facto controller. In England, there was an erosion of monarchial power as the parliament and prime minister both gained influence. As the power and influence of the Papacy waned, other rulers were forced to relinquish power to secular sources and seek their support to prevent total loss. As these newly elevated bourgeoisie classes began to accrue greater control, they began to shift wealth to themselves as well.

The danger in dispelling the divine leadership myth, however, was how best to control the masses now? The peasants would likely have no trouble joining the bourgeoisie in overthrowing the abusive and inconsiderate royalty, as they did in France, but how then would the bourgeoisie implement their own rule? They were not so foolish as to foment a revolution without first having determined a new method for exacting the necessary control over the masses. What better way than by using the dreams and aspirations of the masses against them? Capitalism provided just enough false hope to make it believable.

Let us not be foolish enough to believe the founding fathers of this country were peasants. While many working class people died and sacrificed in the formation of the country, it was designed by and for the bourgeoisie. They quickly elevated themselves to the new ruling class and replaced the monarchies and dictators. These pioneers would be joined later by other elevated bourgeoisie to become the one percent we know today: the controllers of wealth and power. The statistics vary depending upon the resource or parameters one wishes to use but does it make a difference whether it is one percent that controls 80 percent of the wealth or if 3 percent controls 70 percent? The distribution of wealth, in this country and globally, is woefully wanting by moral, ethical, humanitarian, and most religious standards. Suffice to say that I will refer to this segment as the one percent.

So now, instead of monarchies and dictators, we have land-owning elevated bourgeoisie in power. Originally the only people allowed to vote in this country were land owning free white men. Is this a coincidence that this matches the same qualities of those in control? Hardly. Those in power are safely entrenched to maintain that power, even though there is the veil of true democracy. Even today, with the expansion of voters' rights and with the membership of the elite being expanded, it's still a ruse. To run for a seat in Congress, it takes on average $1.7 million. That makes running for Congress just a bit of a stretch for the average American. In this way, the one percent were able to control the sanctity of leadership in much the same way as birthright was used to establish royalty. They were now able to manipulate who was actually eligible or able to become a leader and make it sound more attainable than it actually was. I remember as a boy in school our teachers used to tell us that what made America better than the communists was that anyone could be President. Do you really believe that anyone, regardless of financial status, could be President in this country? Even the "poorest" Presidential candidates with any reasonable chance of success have an estimated net worth around the $300,000 mark. Remember too that these are estimates based on information disclosed by the candidates at their discretion, so they are almost certainly far higher than estimated.

Rather than divine right, the promise of democracy and capitalism is what is now used to keep the masses obedient. The capitalist dream is that if one works hard, one will reap the great rewards of wealth. This is indeed enticing and seems to be a valid possibility at first glance. But I will demonstrate to you how it is and always has been more of a parlor trick than a reality. The true design of capitalism was always as a means to lull the masses into compliance and thus ensure the continued wealth and control by the one percent. Some concessions are made along the way and opportunities are taken advantage of by some, to be sure, but the American Dream for the majority is really just that: a dream. Capitalism fed into the same enticing idea of social mobility as Christianity but with a difference.

A dirty beggar now had the opportunity to gain the same wealth and influence as a wealthy aristocrat, or so they were told. The key difference here is that in order to promise social mobility as an enticement, social distinctions have to be maintained. If we do not continue to hold one class as being inferior, then how then can we classify one as superior? There has to be a reference point for capitalism to work. How can we measure financial success if we can't point to one person who clearly has a smaller house and mathematically less currency than the other person? If we have the controllers of capital employing the laborers, then we need to have people that are flush with capital and those who are not. We cannot have everyone equally rich or equally poor.

So Christianity promises social mobility, with the ultimate objective being the eradication of social distinctions. Capitalism promises social mobility, with the ultimate objective of elevating yourself above as many others as possible. Of course the only way to do this is by ensuring there are people to climb over and this is done by guaranteeing that there will continue to be social classifications. The evolution of the middle income segment was a necessary evil accepted by the one percent. By adding a new rung to the ladder, the rich can offer a means to appease the masses. Now that one segment of the population has the satisfaction of at least being above the lower segment, they are placated. The fear of returning to that status pacifies them through fear of losing what they have gained. Really, it is the same as the circumstance that the old bourgeoisie found themselves in with royalty. It is amazing how sometimes we appear to have come so far and yet we really haven't gone anywhere.

So, on one hand, we have evolved to a point where we no longer ignorantly believe people have a genetic predisposition for superiority or inferiority. Previous to this evolution of thought, an Asian man was considered inferior simply for being an Asian man with no consideration at all to the choices, efforts, or individual qualities of the man. Sadly though, we have slipped from one extreme to the other. Now we dump choice and personal responsibility squarely in people's laps without pause or consideration for the detrimental circumstances in which they may find themselves or the hindrances toward their successful mobility created by the very system we manipulate. Previously, we would say the Asian man was undeserving of the opportunity to accumulate personal wealth or was simply incapable of doing so. Now, we say being born into poverty is no excuse and if a man were truly motivated, he would be just as successful as the man born into a family with massive wealth and influence because socio-economic disadvantage has no relevance. Sure, rising above and overcoming the odds is always a great story but let us not pretend wealth and status have no relevance or that achieving these through will alone is a simple matter possible for anyone. We do accept this indifferent distribution of blame because it is easier to accept than the truth, which is that capitalism ensures not everyone will be equally rich. Stated another way, it means that so many people must be financial "failures" for the system to prevail.

The greatest of all ironies is that the only reason this country was able to develop under such purist capitalist influence is the fact it had access to, or took by force, vast amounts of riches that it then gave away for free. Getting something for nothing, the very antithesis of what we argue for today in the maintenance of capitalism, is exactly what allowed it to flourish in the first place. This country was giving away hundreds of acres to a single person. This is much of what the American Dream was based on. Poor immigrants coming from Europe had an opportunity to own a plot that would be considered large even by many of the wealthiest back home. It was this promise of coming into immediate wealth that lured many and what sustained the dream even for those caught in the oppressive work in the cities. No other country, at the time of its choice to implement capitalism, has had this kind of wealth to throw around so freely, which is why they have all had to do so with higher levels of socialist controls in place. All throughout the world (Canada, South Korea, Finland, Sweden, Germany, etc.), these capitalist nations have profound amounts of socialist policies in place. Free healthcare, retirement benefits, and services which demand their high tax rates. America, on the other hand, went for a long time without any major social programs in place and incredibly low taxes in comparison.

Since the inception of capitalism, the great lure has always been the ability to reach the pinnacle of financial security and self-sustainability. Yet for most of the formative years of this country, that was unattainable except for the exceptionally rare circumstance. Of course a handful of success stories were repeatedly told as further enticement by the educated and wealthy, who knew there was minimal chance for the typical person to achieve the same. Even when this ideal was being blatantly abused and hope was all but nonexistent, the great promise was alluring enough to ignore all logical signs to the contrary.

It was not until the inception of unions and other anti-capitalist concepts that progress began to be made. It became necessary for the one percent to, begrudgingly, make concessions in order to stave off the inevitable revolution predicted by Marx and Engels. By the early twentieth century, the government had stopped giving away huge chunks of land for free. While segregation was in full swing, the freed slaves were still saturating certain segments of the labor market. The hope for the American Dream was all but dead and the deplorable work conditions described by Upton Sinclair were near universal for American laborers. The American populace was so disgusted by the revelation of current practices in the meat packing industry in particular that it actually resulted in a Presidential response. The creation of the FDA and the implementation of standards to that industry were the start of serious social reform. The benefits of concepts that utterly contradict the free market theory are what ultimately spurred the motion of the general populace toward this long sought after goal. As the proliferation of such Altruistically Inspired Societal Economic leaning programs (social security, welfare, labor laws, etc.) and other corrective actions to the failings of the free market (anti-trust regulation, safety standards, minimum wage, etc.) became more expansive, so did the ability of America's proletariat (working segment) to procure more wealth for themselves. Should this really be regarded as a coincidence?

Many have attributed capitalism with sole credit for the formation of the middle income segment. While Adam Smith and John Maynard Keynes have shaped many of the current economic philosophies, capitalism is hardly a modern day product. Depending on which historical reference one chooses to accept and one's definition of capitalism, whether that is micro or macro too, versions of it can be traced back more than 2,000 years ago. It is more widely accepted that modern capitalism finds its roots around the sixteenth century and the development of mercantilism. These considerations make a direct correlation argument murky at best, a mudslide at worst. Even if one wants to point to Adam Smith and the establishment of America as the true beginning of capitalism, executed in a macro-economic level, the direct correlation argument is still extremely weak.

The generally accepted time frame for the wide scale proliferation of the modern middle income segment is from 1945 to 1950. Not only is this roughly 170 years after the creation of conventional capitalism but if we're trying to establish a direct correlation argument, then it seems highly coincidental that the G.I. bill is passed in 1944. This allowed the 12.2 million military personnel (roughly 8.7% of the U.S. population) access to money for tuition, living expenses, mortgages, and to start a business. Don't mistake this reference as negativity toward it because I absolutely support the G.I. bill and honestly think it doesn't do enough. The point here though, is to objectively acknowledge the AISE function of this bill. This bill is not an example of capitalism. Neither are the Social

Security, welfare, and unemployment benefits that were put in place a mere nine years earlier. Can we really attribute the formation of the modern middle income segment with an event that occurred 170 years before its recognized genesis or are we going to cede the credit to four massively financed and nationally executed altruistic programs that occurred less than a decade before? Coincidentally, it should be further noted that many economists recognize it typically takes around a decade for policy changes and implementations to have a realized impact.

Certainly there are other factors that have facilitated and accelerated this growth in wealth. The possession of wealth makes it possible to generate greater wealth and is a cumulative process. This is a basic business concept and is the foundation for every retirement plan. You may only have a hundred dollars but that creates the ability to make more money through the application of compounding interest. This can be greatly accelerated given the proper investment but even at nominal rates of growth it has been proven to reap large rewards. But the genesis of these other factors and what allowed the continuation of this ability to have wealth is the protection of laborers' interests and benefits afforded by these Altruistically Inspired Societal Economic practices. It is not the eventual vehicles or methods that allowed ever increasing levels of wealth to be accrued that are relevant in this part of the discussion but, instead, the acknowledgement that none of it would have been possible without the initial ability of the working class to finally secure some wealth for themselves.

When the one percent was limiting labor growth by demanding each laborer work exhaustively for wages simultaneously driven down by the same labor limiting practice, it was impossible to generate any savings. Employers would pay the lowest wages they could convince a person to work for and demand 12 hour work days. Long work days meant that they could employ less people so there were always people who needed work. Thus, anyone demanding higher wages would be quickly replaced by someone willing to accept those wages, or lower, in place of no wages at all. The inevitable factors of life were ignored by the uncaring one percent, as an injury or illness could and often did, ruin a family. Child labor laws to make educating kids actually feasible, minimum wages to prevent the abhorrent practice of making laborers underbid each other, and other such changes are what made it possible for the American working segment to actually start saving money. With the implementation of social security, people suddenly had more wealth immediately at their disposal. Unions continued to improve working conditions and squeeze more concessions from the one percent. This all helped to set the stage for the 1980's as the middle income group had finally established enough education, wealth, and altruistic legal protections to begin to participate in the system not just as simple laborers any more but as those with real potential to achieve the upward financial mobility so long promised but rarely realized.

This newfound wealth, which provided the middle income segment with unprecedented levels of disposable income as well as leisure time, was the catalyst for sending the consumer economy into overdrive. Consumerism had been increasing steadily as the middle income segment had been growing both in size and in levels of actual wealth but now it could support tremendous amounts of growth. And so the free market responded, as designed, with a massive outpouring of consumer items and services like never before in human history. Sure, examples of excess and leisure are well documented in history but not on this scale and, more importantly, not for such a widespread spectrum of the total society. Previous examples had been isolated in participation to only the miniscule population of the filthy rich of that particular period.

Finally, the capitalist dream had come true. It had taken two hundred years but the suffering of previous generations was worth it to prove that the promises of the free market economy were attainable. Let us not be bothered with the annoying fact that by this time it was the social programs, altruistic concepts, and free market restrictions in place that made any of this possible. The baby boomer generation achieved levels of financial success that their parents, who grew up in the Great Depression, could not even have dreamed of being possible. This prosperity allowed the general populace to finally realize the kinds of luxuries once reserved only for the select few. The capitalist notions became self-perpetuating as greater levels of accumulated wealth gave access to greater levels of consumption which, in turn, demanded greater levels of wealth. From the one percent perspective, it was equally beneficial, for the time being, as this cycle also accelerated their own levels of wealth and availability of contrivances to previously unknown levels.

Soon the recently achieved success of the middle income segment to the level of financial stability seemed empty and irrelevant as now a new level of excess had been established. Forget that at no point in human history had so many people of a singular society known such access to not just food and shelter but totally disposable income to spend on trinkets and baubles. Couple this with unprecedented amounts of leisure time (no more food gathering, hunting, farming, fixing the straw roof, etc.) and one would imagine that this should have been the dawn of the second Renaissance. But there was no overall feeling of satisfaction and enjoyment for this time of free consumption. Instead (and I fail to understand the surprise in this) the highly touted, sought after, and universally practiced capitalist ideals led to ever increasing levels of desire to consume and gather wealth. Isn't this the very basis of capitalism? There is no such thing as enough; it is designed to create a continual search for higher levels of wealth accumulation. This is often erroneously misconstrued as a desire for higher achievement which is true if by "achievement" you mean wealth accumulation.

As one analyzes the psychological evolution of the last three or four generations, one can see how each successive generation is coming to the same conclusion, each a little more quickly than the last. The baby boomers did not come into their wealth until they had achieved working maturity and from there it grew steadily. Their lack of catharsis could be excused as it had not had time to sink in yet or, more likely, they had not quenched the consumption desire yet. The answer of course was to consume more, which they did. My generation grew up with more, initially, than our parents. It is almost as if the availability of consumption grew as I grew. So the excuse for the lack of catharsis could be put off because we could never quite catch up to the evolution of consumption possibilities. The 8-track gave way to the tape deck, then the Walkman, then the CD player. The constant evolution of products to consume was like the proverbial carrot on a stick. The answer of course was to consume more, which we did. When you look at millennials, you see they have been inundated with baubles, trinkets, and distractions from birth. The proliferation of new products has slowed in terms of their awe inspiring originality. When you grow up with a talking phone, 3D TV, and 24 hour access to global data on a tablet, it becomes difficult to elicit real amazement. This generation has already experienced more consumer excess than the previous two combined, so their lack of catharsis has left them floundering for an answer.

What we are all beginning to realize, at different stages for each individual group, but collectively at the same time, is that there is a moral chasm we long to fill. This is the catharsis for which we are starting to search as we all begin to realize, through personal experience of trial and error, that no amount of trinkets or distractions can bring us the release we seek. Most people have not come to overtly recognize it in these straightforward terms but the signs are all there. Like addicts, we've been consuming voraciously, looking for the ultimate purchase that finally satiates our appetite. However, that catharsis isn't going to come from materialism; it's going to come from doing what we know is morally correct.

Effective Propaganda

*Nothing in the world is more
dangerous than sincere ignorance
and conscientious stupidity.*

Martin Luther King Jr.

Funny how supporting capitalism is oddly linked to the perception of supporting nationalism even though capitalism knows no national boundaries, as is clearly evidenced by the exporting of jobs overseas for no reason other than cheaper labor and lower tax brackets. This is just another form of propaganda and control. By linking capitalism with ideas of nationalism, it makes criticism of the former more difficult by muddling the conversation with tangents irrelevant to the core of the discussion. If one criticizes capitalism, one must also be unpatriotic...even though capitalism itself is unpatriotic. Minimal to no consideration is given to national security issues caused by becoming over-reliant upon foreign entities for labor, production sites, or even specific skills. The one percent, however, does not want anyone pointing out that the emperor is not wearing any clothes. For the longest time in this country, some of the most patriotic professions a kid could aspire to were police officer, firefighter, or soldier. Guess what? Those are all publicly funded and therefore only possible as an AISF ideal.

The H-1B program was designed so employers could temporarily fill vacancies caused by a lack of qualified indigenous people, specifically in positions requiring a minimum of a bachelor's degree. It has been a common complaint, particularly in the IT industry, that employers have been misusing the program to replace American workers with cheaper foreign labor. The H-1B rules make it clear that visa workers are to be paid the prevailing wage to prevent the displacement of American workers. This means businesses are required to pay these foreign workers the same amount they would normally pay. From a business perspective, the question is then why pay the application fees and assume the responsibility for travel expenses, as is required, if the cost of wages is not going to be any lower? In addition, the company also assumes an ethical and business responsibility to assist in the acclimation of these new temporary employees. One must also account for financial loss due to the transitional period of a new worker learning the proper procedures and for them to become acclimated in their personal lives to the new culture and surroundings.

All the businesses making use of this program insist they are adhering to the law and paying foreign workers the same wages they would have paid an American worker. If that is true, then this hiring action lacks sound business sense from a purely financial aspect. It should be further noted that reports show 55% of American graduates with a technical degree are currently working in a non-related occupation. If the spirit of the law is being upheld, then all costs associated with the employment of the visa worker should exceed the cost of employing an American worker, with the addition of all other costs noted above. It makes no business sense to undertake these added expenses under these assumptions when there are already indigenous employees capable of performing the work. Yet despite these public statistics and simple mathematical calculations, large American businesses continually push Congress to increase the current cap on the number of applications allowable through the H-1B program. Although there has been no definitive evidence proving misuse of the H-1B program by any company, the straightforward mathematics make use of the program by strict adherence to its regulations, at best, difficult to believe. It is generally supported that anyone who speaks out against the benefits of capitalism is deemed un-American but when it comes to exploiting every possible cost-cutting measure by fully embracing capitalism, there apparently are no national boundaries.

Democracy and capitalism are two separate concepts, yet I have read business articles where the author refers to the "democratization" of a business due to deregulation. When you break it down, this statement makes no sense. Deregulating an industry does not make it more democratic. Deregulation of the airlines did not lead to passengers getting to vote on ticket prices or destination routes because *that* would be democratization. Deregulation allows the controllers of capital (owners, CEOs, etc.) to manage the individual companies within the industry with less, or no, oversight or restriction. How in the world is this considered democracy? While it is true the controllers of capital then have greater freedom in how and what they wish to do, so does a dictator. Greater freedom by those in control does not define democracy. Instead, it is supposed to be freedom by the masses to make decisions based on a majority that defines it. That majority may be by 1 single vote or by 1 billion votes, which many people forget. As much as people clamor about the freedom and equality and greatness of democracy, they often forget that as much 49.9% of the population stands to be alienated by the final decision. Don't get me wrong, democracy is good; let's just not pretend it is synonymous with bliss or freedom for that matter. In accordance with a democracy, as long as 50.1% of the people vote one way, I am obligated to abide by that decision. I don't have the freedom to ignore that decision, even if I hate it, because if I do they have a different name for that. It's called anarchy.

Deregulation allows the decisions of those in control to become based purely on profit, the core of the free market economy, because they no longer need to account for extraneous stipulations. That is a simple supply and demand relationship that has nothing to do with democracy. Yet such verbiage is interlaced so as to continue the incorrect thought that capitalism, democracy, and freedom are somehow all the same thing. Like some weird re-imagination of the Holy Trinity.

The fact remains that these are three completely separate theories.

Stating that democracy is better than socialism is like saying that Ford trucks are better than the color blue. This is because democracy is a form of governing system and socialism is an economic system. You might say, "What's the difference?" but the relationship between economics and government mirrors the relationship between cooking and physical health. You can eat nothing but the absolute best, certified, stamped, approved, grade A, super-triple-organic, best-stuff-on-Earth food, but if you smoke a pack of cigarettes while sitting on your ass watching crappy reality television all day, you're not going to be healthy. Conversely, you can't expect to go to the gym four hours a day, do yoga, meditation, and get spa treatments, and think that a Cheetos-only diet is going to achieve perfect health either. So what you cook and how you cook it plays an integral part in your overall health but there are also plenty of other factors to be accounted for. How much sleep you get, what your stress levels are, how physically demanding your profession is, your mental and emotional stability, and many other facets play a part in how healthy you will be. So you can't really discuss a person's health without including, to some degree, their diet and how they cook it as well as other facets too.

So I would never refer to someone graduating from culinary school as a medical professional because I realize that while the two topics are intertwined, they are not synonymous. The same applies to economics and government. Of course a government needs to decide how it will regulate the economy of its society- whether it is free market, socialist, or AISE. Yet as intertwined as the two facets are, they are not one and the same. Rome went from a republic to a dictatorship but the economy did not convert to socialism. According to the misguided perceptions we hold today, shouldn't that have *had* to happen?

Stalin, Castro, or Kim Jong-il imprisoning and executing their citizens has nothing to do with the economic systems employed in their respective countries. It makes them despots and dictators. It should also be recognized here that it has become popular to praise the excellent healthcare system in Cuba. Their healthcare system is a prime example of the benefits of Altruistically Inspired Societal Economics, *despite* the vicious and dictatorial rule of Castro. The success of Cuba's healthcare system was not dependent on Castro's style of leadership. A dictatorship is not necessary to implement the same beneficial healthcare system elsewhere. Such erroneous praise for Castro only serves to create an unwarranted and negative correlation between AISE and oppression. Finland, Canada, Sweden, and Denmark employ highly socialist practices. They do so with extremely high tax rates and, in turn, put in place programs that ensure the wellbeing of all their citizens. The truth is that much of what we think we know about socialism is actually highly effective propaganda to get us to submissively buy into capitalism. Which coincidently helps to maintain the power and wealth of those disbursing the propaganda.

> *The democracy will cease to exist*
> *when you take away from those*
> *who are willing to work and give to*
> *those who would not.*

Thomas Jefferson

The preceding quote is true, to an extent, regardless of whether one attempts to practice laissez-faire (hands off) capitalism, our current pseudo-socialist capitalism, or AISE. As I have made clear previously, democracy cannot logically be a counter point to socialism and so, in this manner, Jefferson is wrong. Democracy has nothing to do with whether or not people work. It has to do with whether or not people vote. Jefferson, belonging to the original one percent, points out something that is true but twists it to make you love capitalism and hate socialism. AISE is not about feeding the lazy and, as a point of fact, isn't that what we do currently? When you consider it, both the one percent and the "professionally unemployed" take from those who work and the negative impact is painfully clear. The problem is that we have been provided an infantile interpretation of AISE that no rational person could accept, precisely because it is not rational. Jefferson was certainly no fool. He knew he was writing effective literature to support the very system that ensured his own financial success. It is difficult for us to comprehend since we have been misled for so long by effective propaganda such as this, but the truth of AISE is that its strength lies in people willingly working for the benefit of all. I will endeavor to expose the truth through the obfuscations.

Originally, the stated purpose of socialism was the abolition of bourgeoisie privately owned resources and ultimately to stop the exploitation of the many by the few. That means they wanted to strip the filthy rich of their control over the overwhelming majority of the wealth and prevent this small percentage of the populace from taking advantage of the majority any further. Does this sound familiar? How could this possibly be interpreted as "the government breaking into homes, seizing personal property, jailing innocents, slaughtering dissidents, and using oppression and fear to control?" There is never even a remote reference to the abolition or removal of self-made property in the *Communist Manifesto*. The only issue that socialism seeks to rectify is that of the wage labor results. AISE isn't about kicking in your front door to take back the seashells your kid collected at the beach, the painting you created, or your grandmother's cannoli recipe.

That is the lie we have been fed by those who want to maintain their control. Listening to the controllers of capital tell us about the evil of socialism is like taking dating advice from a jilted ex. If we all stop bickering amongst ourselves and demand that wealth be equitably reallocated, the one percent stand to lose all their opulence and influence. Do you really think they want us to start thinking that way? Do you think they are above lying and obscuring the truth to prevent this from happening?

This is not a conspiracy theory; it is the obvious truth. Nothing I was ever taught about socialism is actually true and capitalism is really designed to help rich people make more money.

Here are a few more examples of effective propaganda. Since our earliest exposure to American history, we have been taught that capitalism beat fascism in WW II. Incorrect. Opponents might try to take this opportunity to make false and illogically attained leaps and claim that this demonstrates disrespect to America. That is not the case at all and if anyone believes that our Greatest Generation was represented in that era, it is me. This has nothing to do with being anti-American. I have the utmost respect for the generation that sacrificed so much and endured such hardship in the effort to fight the Axis forces. My argument seeks instead to dispel the misleading idea that we have been spoon fed: the false claim that the economic practice of capitalism was a major factor in America's success in WW II.

Americans willingly, enthusiastically, and patriotically volunteered and donated to aluminum drives, rubber drives, and more. They accepted government imposed rationing. There were many Red Cross volunteers and others who donated supplies to the Red Cross. The draft was willingly accepted by the American public and complaining about the draft or trying to avoid it were both considered to be un-American. Government bonds were a terrible investment in terms of return, yet Americans put a lot of money into buying war bonds. The government was giving weapons and supplies to its allies without charging them and with the realization that these countries would likely also be in no position to pay for them after the war. Which is exactly what happened. People and businesses that sought to drive up prices or rates, acting as profiteers, were not popular to say the least. With the level of demand by the U.S. government for weapons and ammunition, manufacturers could have easily charged triple their prices but this did not happen because the public backlash would have been terrible.

All of these highly laudable sacrifices and actions that were necessary to help make winning the war possible are altruistic. All the aforementioned activities are blatantly anti-capitalism. How is volunteering embracing capitalism? How is suffering government imposed rationing and drafting of people capitalism? Excuses can and probably will be made about how sometimes in extreme circumstances exceptions need to be made. Perhaps, but that still does not change the fact that the claim of capitalism defeating fascism is totally false. I view it as further demonstration that, extenuating circumstances or not, this large capitalist nation practiced a considerable level of Altruistically Inspired Societal Economics for a prolonged period of time and did so successfully.

Here is another example of effective propaganda: capitalism beat communism in the Cold War. Incorrect. Again, this is a fine opportunity to accuse me of being anti-American. However, this has nothing to do with being un-American and everything to do with dispelling the misleading propaganda that makes the false claim that the economic practice of capitalism was the main factor in America's success in the Cold War. Asian strategy has historically relied upon a dependence on sheer numbers for military effectiveness, from the Mongols to the Chinese to the Russians. When the Soviets chose to embrace this approach, they executed it by mass producing low-tech equipment. This allowed them to quickly and cheaply produce incredible amounts of armaments and supplies. This was a decision made and executed by an oligarchy to destructively focus the massive majority of the national economy toward weapons manufacture. Their ideology was based on exerting oppressive and threatening rule over the country, while discouraging education or free thinking. None of this has anything to do with socialist economics.

These are not AISE ideals, but simply the particular ideals of this group of ruthless leaders who cloaked themselves in the title of socialists. This served to limit their capacity to discover intellectual talent. Those who were academically gifted and did not feel a misplaced need to be loyal to these falsely declared socialists fled, knowing that they would be rewarded with asylum in the U.S. for their talents. The secondary effect of choosing to research and develop sophisticated technology with the primary intent of producing highly effective armaments in limited quantities is that the benefits of the new technology eventually gets passed on to the civilian populace. The internet, medical breakthroughs, and helicopters are just a few examples of this effect. The Soviets had limited technological gains to pass on to their populace because they had not made many. Although they were not highly inclined to do so anyway, the concept still applies. The technological advances made by the U.S., which are arguably the real source of the victory, are not attributable to capitalism but instead to the lack of oppression. It was the choice of quality over quantity, the difference between an oppressed state versus a free state, and the poor economic decisions by usurpers of authority that won the Cold War.

There have been numerous catch phrases that have caught on over the years to innocuously keep people in alignment with capitalist ideals. For example, "It's just business." This is a popular saying that many people like to throw around when referring to someone else's situation. When you can't provide for your family, it gets personal very quickly. The only time it is not personal is when you need to justify doing something you know to be otherwise wrong or devoid of human consideration. This saying is just a subversive application of propaganda so people do not need to bear the guilt of carrying out the merciless necessities of capitalism. Sorry, you're two days overdue so we're going to evict you, but it's just business. Sorry, I have to destroy your credit for not paying the ludicrous amount of medical bills and I'm sorry your mom died, but it's just business. Sorry, I have to lay you off. Management thought the team-building retreat expense was more important than being able to keep you employed, but it's just business. When you're on the giving end of these scenarios, it's just business. When you're on the receiving end, it's very personal.

"You should be grateful for your job." I despise this phrase. It is the quintessential one percent mindset used to threaten the proletariat (worker) into submission. It reveals the ugly truth of the lack of compassion by the controllers of capital not openly discussed in text books regarding capitalism. It actually has nothing to do with real free market economics. The laborer is supposed to simply fulfill a need that the owner of capital wishes to satisfy. To his credit, this is idealistically described by Adam Smith as a symbiotic relationship wherein neither the owner of production nor the laborer can profitably survive without the participation of the other. Therefore the owner of the means of production, in theory, should be equally grateful to the laborer for performing the task.

Smith does not state or imply that the laborer is to be manipulated or taken advantage by the owner. It is Smith's contention, presented in the *Wealth of Nations*, that if the working conditions or more specifically, the compensation is considered sub-par, then the free market forces simply allow the worker to choose a different employer. Now whether Smith actually believed this or if he simply chose not to publicly acknowledge that the owner can and should exploit the workers is unknown. After all, he wrote the book with the full intention of publishing it and dispersing it widely. My point is that despite what he wrote, who is to say that Smith actually believed this idealistic relation between laborer and owner or that he secretly knew and supported the inevitable contemptuous relationship. Further, as I note in the next chapter, he certainly has no problem with business owners manipulating the system to the detriment of the consumer who, for all intents and purposes, is also the laborer.

The reality is that by threatening the laborer's livelihood, the owners are able to exact control and submission. Demeaning the laborer, making them believe they should be grateful for their job, makes it more likely the laborer will accept decreases in wages, loss of benefits, increased workloads, or degraded work conditions with a docile reaction. This is the application of proven psychology seen in abusive relationships. There are volumes of texts that outline this very practice of behavioral control by the use of carefully selected, and usually baseless, verbal degradation. I'm sorry, I had the understanding that I *chose* this job so I could perform specified tasks with the simple promise of compensation through an agreed upon rate of monetary reimbursement; not that I came groveling through the door, beholden to the prospective employer and ever grateful for their charitable payment of wages for my labors.

Consider the words carefully. You should be grateful for your job. It is not just the seven words that are spoken but the deeper and socially accepted implications associated with those words. A job in many ways defines who you are as a person in this country. If someone says that guy is a minister, typically and not totally unjustly, certain assertions and assumptions are immediately made. Used car salesman, defense attorney, doctor; these job titles also are usually used to estimate a person's financial worth or at least their earning/spending potential. While the "professionally unemployed" sector is growing in this country, those who work do so, in part, because having a job is still considered not just necessary but respectable. A job also represents a means of generating the resources to provide for one's family which is, and should be, a strong source of pride for many. Conversely, the absence of a job means the inability to provide properly.

So this phrase now says that you should be grateful/obliged/thankful/indebted/gratified to the employer for providing you with purpose/dignity/identity/pride/respect/usefulness. Wow. Now I feel like an absolute degenerate for having the audacity to complain, instead of showing the requisite amount of deference and gratitude the employer thinks I should be feeling and displaying. The threat of a $1.00 per hour wage cut also doesn't concern me as much since I now have the subconscious connection to all the intangible aspects that are still being conferred upon me by my employer. Because if I quit or get fired, I then lose purpose/dignity/identity/pride/respect/usefulness which I had, only as a direct result of what my employer made possible for me. Sounds pretty sick, doesn't it? Altruistically Inspired Societal Economics does not have this abusive psychological manipulation, nor does it require it.

It has been reported that the 62 wealthiest people on Earth have as much combined wealth as the poorest 50 percent of the world, which comes to about 3.6 billion people. How can we read a statistic like that and still say that we support capitalism? How can anything good come from this? I can't find a way to justify this figure in any way, shape, or form that is humanitarian or spiritual. Why would any one of these 62 people want to see AISE put into place? More importantly, why are we all supporting capitalism and continuing to argue amongst ourselves over fiscal issues when these 62 people are allowed to live care free? If we continue to stand idly by, complacent in our own comfort while millions of people needlessly suffer and starve, we stand as guilty as those who gorge themselves on the opulence their wealth buys.

> *When I say unto the wicked, O wicked man, thou shalt surely die; if thou dost not speak to warn the wicked from his way, that wicked man shall die in his iniquity; but his blood will I require at thine hand.*
>
> Ezekiel 33:8

Adam Smith: Biggest Supporter of the One Percent

No one has ever become poor from giving.

Anne Frank

The ever increasing prevalence of the mega-corporation provides additional proof of the false presumptions about capitalism. Where is the supposed free market competition? Oh, that's right. That entire ludicrous concept is based on identical items being sold. All the technical, academic, intellectually stimulating, fanciful, and theoretical assumptions of free market economics are based on identical goods and services being offered. It ignorantly assumes that if one provider finds a more efficient manner of production there will be a short-lived imbalance before all other competitors quickly implement the exact same changes. The first obvious problem with this is that the whole system is predicated upon theories formulated in the extreme infancy of the industrial revolution, if not before. *An Inquiry Into the Nature and Causes of the Wealth of Nations* was published in 1776 but took Smith an estimated nine years to write it. Depending on whose interpretation one chooses to accept, the industrial revolution didn't begin until roughly 1760. It is one thing to make this simple assumption of how the market will quickly and efficiently respond to new products based on an economic system where hand carved wooden spoons are being sold. However, there is no way Smith could have conceptualized the current level of complexity, not only in the scope of differing types of goods and services available but specifically in the levels of multifaceted differentiation within each of those specific goods and services.

While home computers are ubiquitous today, there are still many ways in which the varying producers differentiate themselves and their products from each other. Not only do certain companies have a reputation for specific strengths or weaknesses but the way in which you choose products is different. There are also differences in the quality of materials used, the production processes, the choice to use bottom cost labor or not, quality control methods, and many other aspects. Today, there are numerous factors influencing purchase choices that have nothing to do with the product itself. For instance, there are many people who continued to buy Craftsman tools, despite some opining a drop in quality, because of the long standing policy of no-hassle returns. Some didn't mind a possibly inferior quality tool as long as it could be replaced without hassle. The no hassle return has a reputation that was built over decades. Toyota has a long history of safety and quality but is also recognized for their exceptional marketing skill and defect-free efficient production. Many people support Costco, despite potential price differences, because the company is known for being responsible to and supportive of its employees. High quality customer service often influences consumers to purchase items at higher prices or even inferior quality because of the peace of mind that it offers in the future.

Certainly there are some identical goods and services in the market place. And while some are identical in the literal sense, others are similar enough that the only factor affecting purchase selection is price. Gasoline is one such example of the latter as the product itself is so regulated that it is, for all intents and purposes, identical. Most gas stations in a geographic locale will charge identical prices. But that being said, being closer to the highway or where there is easier access to and from the particular station can justify an increase of $.10 a gallon. So while identical goods do exist to a limited extent, the current factors that affect purchase decisions are vastly more complex than the outdated theories proposed by Adam Smith. However, the existing system and future estimations are still based upon these outdated assumptions and models.

Smith, while explaining the benefits of corporations, clearly acknowledges that members of one industry might be forced to buy goods at a higher price because of the necessary agreement to buy from fellow members of the same town-corporate. This means that the lumber yard might need to charge the dentist more to build his new office because they have a smaller forest area than the next town over, thereby making lumber more costly. The dentist promises to use this lumber yard though because he needs to support a fellow local business owner, just as he expects the lumber yard owner to use his dental services. Now there are certain understandable elements to this unity that ensure the vitality of the overall local market. If the lumber yard went out of business, it would also negatively impact the dentist as a town that can't support a lumber yard is likely not going to attract more people and businesses to move there. Fewer businesses mean even less people residing in the town which means less people seeking dental services. So the two business owners make a mutually beneficial pact to support each other, thereby making the entire town-corporate more attractive to future business prospects and keeping current businesses operating as well. This is all well and good but the reality is that the dentist must raise his rates to make up for the need to pay a higher cost for lumber to build his house and office.

This is acceptable, according to Smith, because all the business owners can charge a higher price since the other members are equally obligated to purchase from them. Therefore, the baker must increase his rates, since he has to pay more for dental work and lumber, and so on and so forth for all the other business operators in this particular town-corporate. So where exactly is the benefit that Smith outlines? If everyone charges an inflated rate to each other, then the consumer (the laborers) are inundated with inflated prices throughout their specific market. One can make the argument that eventually wages in this locale will have to increase to adjust for these inflated prices. This is true, but it means that every time the controlling one percent choose to artificially inflate prices, the laborers lose until such time that their wages catch up to "market fluctuations."

This process still happens today but now it is not just collusion among independent tradesmen. Today we see this involvement in the form of the aforementioned mega-corporations. One enormous company owns hundreds of subsidiaries, usually in a purposefully convoluted array of legal clouding. If subsidiary A needs services or resources from subsidiary B, a discount offered by B would just diminish B's bottom line. Sometimes this is done intentionally to produce accounting magic but it is better for B to simply charge what it wants to A and then pass that cost to A's customers. This is actually worse than the situation that Smith suggested, in that at least he was referring to independent business owners colluding for mutual gain. However, the scenario above entails one mega-corporation garnering the positive effects from both companies synergistically.

As a point of fact, inflation in this country is carefully controlled but not just to hold it in check as best as possible, as many might assume. Instead, the Federal Reserve does what it can to make sure there is always a little bit of inflation for the very same purpose as discussed above. The artificial creation of inflation ensures that prices are constantly increasing. This generates increased profitability, as wage increases always lag behind price increases. So, for the entire time between price increase and wage increase (for all separate workforce elements), the one percent generate higher profits while getting their labor for the same cost. When one studies the relationship of prices and inflation, it is quite evident that this is nothing more than a convoluted process with the sole design of allowing the one percent to generate greater wealth. The loaf of bread costs $2.00 now instead of $.25, not because it is scarcer now or more desirable than it used to be, but because of the mathematical machinations designed to increase profitability. The result that goes unnoticed by most is that it is not just a simple proportional increase of both price and wage. Yes, as raises occur, a new level of equilibrium is attained. But for the entire time before you and every other laborer involved in the process gets that raise, the corporation is reaping greater profitability.

As an analogy, let's say you and the owner are driving in separate cars. The owner is exactly one mile ahead of you and both of you are driving at 20 mph. Every ten miles, the owner accelerates by 1 mph but you are made to wait an additional one mile before you are able to make that same acceleration of 1 mph. This means that after every ten miles, the owner is able to slowly pull further ahead of you for one full mile. When you are able to accelerate, it seems as though equilibrium has been established because you are in fact driving at the same speed again. But the owner is getting further and further ahead each time he reaches the advanced acceleration point. Every time the owners raise prices, they are getting richer and we are getting poorer until wage increases occur. We are lulled into a sense of stability that is not true and, more importantly, not unintentional.

Economics is not physics. There are some mathematical realities but, by and large, the system only works because we are willing to accept the given parameters. We cannot just choose to ignore the laws of gravity or make sound travel faster than light but we can choose to stop accepting inflation. This choice is a reality most people do not understand and that the one percent employ to exploit the workers for ever-increasing wealth accumulation. This is how the one percent continue to get richer even as prices rise across all sectors. If this were not true, then as prices rose due to inflation everyone would simply maintain their relative position of wealth in relationship to one another.

When the suppliers of industry control enough of the market related to a good or service for which there is no reasonable alternative (i.e.: food, energy), they can assert their will upon the system and defy the demand of the people. This also relates back to Smith acknowledging how business owners in his own time had the ability to manipulate prices, in direct contradiction to the supply and demand paradigm. It would be easy to explain the lack of the theoretical supply and demand response with convoluted excuses regarding politics or extenuating circumstances, but the truth is the failing is embedded in capitalism itself. To blame the failings of the free market system on politics is to not understand the free market actually relies on government and, thus, politics. In other words, free market capitalism cannot exist without the assistance of the government guiding and protecting it. Yet a government that relies on capitalism is then at too much risk of falling victim to the traps of capitalism, thereby making its failing inevitable. I cover this in a subsequent chapter.

Smith openly admits that at practically every assembly of those of a common trade, these tradesmen collude to the detriment of the public. His wily solution to this is to not enforce regulations that would occasion any additional assemblies by common tradesmen. Wow. Not one utterance or suggestion to stave off or eliminate this practice which is in direct conflict with his own theories. This lauded economist's solution is: don't have these guys get together any more than necessary. Problem solved. If this was not the basis for the very system we rely upon to guarantee our ability to provide for ourselves, it would be laughable. Yet this is the problem we see incessantly from Smith. He clearly favors the monetary gain of the one percent at every turn, but somehow we have been convinced this same system is the saving grace for the rest of us to find financial success.

Smith further acknowledges this collusion is in the best interest of the tradesmen and is thus employed whenever possible. One method employed to accomplish this was to purposefully ensure an availability of skilled tradesman that was less than what the market actually requires. This was executed by limiting not only the number of tradesmen but also the number of apprentices that would be taken on. For example, if a town had an expected amount of business that would keep a blacksmith and two apprentices busy working twelve hours a day, the associated guild would agree to only allow one blacksmith and one apprentice working twelve hours a day. This was to ensure there would always be greater demand than supply of services. In this way, people would be willing to pay more to expedite the completion of their own projects and the blacksmith would have steady work all the time. Smith is indifferent to the inconvenience of the populace or the unnecessary spike in price. Some would call this smart business management. So, if you have acute appendicitis but there is only one overworked doctor in town because of the application of "smart business management," will you still feel the same? Let's not forget that the common defense of capitalism is its great benefit to us, the working segment. So defending these obviously detrimental practices does not make sense. This is another example of how capitalism serves the profitable interests of the one percent at the cost of the convenience and desire of society.

Smith in fact acknowledges, even in these simpler times, that those in control of supply can affect the supply and demand paradigm to the detriment of the consumer for their own purpose of inflated profitability. To deny this truth seems futile, as one can clearly see in the examples provided that there is sufficient demand to warrant greater supply than is currently available. Of course, we now see this on a much grander scale. Currently, four major air carriers control 90% of the U.S. domestic market share, down from the twenty plus carriers that existed less than a decade ago. For the most part, each airline controls specific hubs within the country and it appears they are content not to engage in price or sale competition. While collusion is almost impossible to prove, even just a feeling of malaise toward competitive pricing amongst all the major players has the exact same effect: insulation to the effects of demand.

It should be noted that the airlines got into a self-immolating price war a few years ago under the foolish pretense that whichever airline offered the lowest cost would then also sell the most tickets and make the most money. They completely ignored the break point at which it actually costs more to do business than not to do business at all. Some might say that this is an example of the system working. It obviously was not as most of the airlines went bankrupt. Bankruptcies put a major strain and burden on the system, people lose their jobs, and contracts are terminated. Price wars are always destructive and there are typically only losers, except in situations such as what happened with Rockefeller. But he intentionally engineered his price war for oil and his company was substantial enough to easily absorb the losses. He accepted, that by absorbing losses for the short term, he would effectively create a monopoly for himself in the end and thus make profitability a certainty in the future. And that is precisely what he did. Generally speaking though, price wars end badly for everyone.

The truth is that everyone knows when supply and demand really do meet, as they theoretically always should, it still creates an undesirable situation. As competitors lower their prices to meet the demands of the consumers, they obviously need to cut costs to maintain profitability. Supposing these competitors are not as foolish as the airlines and choose instead to respect the breakeven point, they should stay just above the point where it actually becomes more costly to continue operations than to shut down. This means the manufacturers are now producing just enough goods at the highest price that consumers are willing to pay for that level of supply. The ugly underside to this harmoniously wonderful balance is that manufacturers will now only pay the lowest wages possible to achieve these levels. The funny thing is that, economics major or not, everyone realizes this but somehow still complains about the lack of a satisfactory wage increase. We want capitalism. We defend capitalism. But we incomprehensibly complain about the effects of capitalism.

The restaurant industry is a prime example of this problem. Profit margins are razor thin and so there is little room to allow for increased wages or worker compensation. It is an industry that most people acknowledge inadequately compensates its employees but yet this fact seems to be readily accepted. Excuses are made for the use of illegal, low-cost workers. The generosity of tipping is celebrated as another solution. We tell this whole segment of the work force to go ahead and accept an insufficient pittance as a salary and count on society to tip you well enough to make up for it. We tolerate it because that is how it is. We know these workers cannot exist on the compensation their occupation provides them, yet we do nothing about it except complain and meekly support them with words.

I'm not ignorant to the many other aspects of taxes, coding regulations, and liquor licensing hurdles that exist and do realize these also hinder profitability in the food service industry. But these issues exist for the whole industry which makes it an even playing field for everyone in it, thus irrelevant in the discussion of competition and free market effects. If every sprinter is saddled with 10% of their body weight on their back, then while their overall times will suffer, all those within the field of racers that day are equally burdened. The point is that if there were less competition, the less controlling forces would be able to dictate supply, and thus price, with greater influence than a wide field of competitors. Of course this would not be good for the consumer. So, ironically, it is the fact the restaurant industry has widespread competition, an integral aspect of the free market system, which makes it so difficult to be profitable. So once again, we see how the consumer is satiated with low cost and wide variety but the producer of goods and services has to struggle for survival. The alternative is that the consumer must accept the set prices and supply or forego the service altogether because the producers are few in number and dictate their rate of profitability, at least to a certain extent.

By removing profitability as the key by which the business remains open and the goods or services are made available for consumption, things become simpler. Many people erroneously believe this is where the state rushes in, declares that brussel sprouts on a stick will be the only food sold, and proceeds to beat anyone who complains. This is not Altruistically Inspired Societal Economics. It is not the solution or recommendation. Thank you Hollywood for the ludicrous, and now pervasive, perception made popular via propagandist efforts to subvert the acceptance of the idea of altruistic economics. Lack of choice is not mutually exclusive with AISE.

Commonality and uniformity are more efficient and require less waste; this is a fact. When it is necessary to implement restraints on waste and decrease inefficiency, of course this will then be the first and fastest solution. This is true regardless of the economic system of choice. Even in capitalism, not everything will be produced to accommodate everyone's desires. I longingly remember Vanilla Cookie Crisp cereal from my childhood. Despite searching in every locale where I have ever lived, I have only been able to find Chocolate Chip Cookie Crisp. Yet this has no bearing on my feelings about capitalism. Even in capitalism, there is a limit to the amount of variety that can be supported, yet it is not a generalized and irrational fear. In capitalism or AISE, I guarantee that others will have to bear the loss of their own Vanilla Cookie Crisp.

AISE is envisioned as functioning within democracy, and it can positively do so. It can also work within the governing system of a republic, which is what this country is. This means that a majority of the people or a majority of those elected to decide for the people, can determine the breadth and depth of variety that will be found in the marketplace. This does not need to be uniformly applied, as a variety of housing options would be expected to garner greater support for individuality than, say, insisting on 700 color variations of video coaxial cables. The restraints on variety would not be based on arbitrary declarations from a faceless dictator, as we have been conditioned to fear. But the constraints would be logically based upon what the society demanded be made available, in conjunction with balancing choices with other matters and the availability of the required resources.

This really doesn't differ drastically from the current format. CEOs don't require a vote from consumers to determine what products they will or will not continue to produce. These decisions are based on focus group data, sales history, and current costs of production. There is a reason there are no coconut flavored, grapefruit infused, jalapeno crusted granola bars. It has nothing to do with an imaginary, soul-crushing, monotonous, and evil communist oppression. It has to do with capitalists realizing there is no value in the production of such a bar. Capitalism does not ensure limitless variety and so AISE need not be held to that standard either.

Don't television shows with a limited following get cancelled every year? It's not as if even the worst show doesn't have at least a handful of loyal followers and fans. So by cancelling the show, is this an example of capitalism emulating the worst characteristics of an imagined version of communism? No, it is a logical reallocation of resources. One thing that capitalism excels at is that it does not tolerate waste. If it is not profitable, laissez faire (hands off) capitalism does not provide for continuing that process. One of the most famous examples of consumer influence is getting Coca Cola to return its original formula to the shelves. This, of course, is purely based upon expected profitability generated by the change and has worked in a number of examples. There have also been similar campaigns for other shows and products which lacked an expectation of profitability that have failed. The reality here is that if there were sufficient excess, such fringe products and services could actually survive in AISE. This is because the burden of profitability would not exist; only majority approval for the utilization of available resources to make it so would be required. The bottom line is that in capitalism, if it does not produce a profit, the particular enterprise is abandoned. In AISE, profit is not a consideration, only availability of the necessary resources and the desire of society to see it delivered is necessary.

So, while touting and establishing the details of one economic system, Smith recognizes and supports actions that stand in direct violation of the same theories he concurrently praises. Now local business owners collude to purchase from each other, despite the availability of other cheaper options, and agree to artificially manipulate prices. Smith has now established two thoughts here, both of which highly favor those in control of supply and contradict his own preaching of free market. He not only describes but also justifies the practice of inflating prices to the consumer for the benefit of those in control of supply. There is absolutely no consideration by Smith as to the negative effect on the consumers by this price inflation. He only defends the necessity of the practice for the wellbeing of the one percent.

He similarly only gives consideration to the positive and, in his estimation, necessary effects on businesses for the practice of collusion in creating shortages of skilled labor demands. He fails to give proper voice to how this is diametrically opposed to his own theories and how this is detrimental to the local consumers. Can you recognize how this still applied practice is detrimental to the consumer and working segment of society? How many openly recognized practices in capitalism give distinct advantage to the one percent and handicap, if not incapacitate, the working segment into a position to be exploited? How much truth does it take for us to realize this system is not, in fact, supportive of the masses and working segment as we have been led to believe? By eliminating the capitalist mentality, there is no need to inflate prices, meaning put more money into the pockets of the one percent.

Smith recognizes the fault of capitalism is that it favors the less skilled industrial worker and tradesmen, due to the effect of incorporation of the trade. The farmer or country laborer is looked down upon, even though he requires a greatly broader amount of knowledge and expertise to achieve his goals. The farmer needs to know about weather, animal husbandry, fertilization, planting, irrigation, a plethora of different machines, and more. The copy machine repair person only needs to know one focused area of ability. Those who operate in more rural settings also often need a wider variety of skills as they usually must be self-sufficient. It is more common for those in a city setting to be more dependent on the multitude of resources easily available to them. Why cook when you pass two dozen eateries on the way home? When one lives in an urban setting, one is far less likely to need to develop skills in maintaining or repairing common household maintenance needs, nor deal with landscaping of any kind. Of course, there are many preconceived social stigmas involved in this subject as well.

Many middle income segment workers are quick to defend capitalism out of pride for their own accomplishments within it. They want to defend their worth versus the burger-flipper or, worse, the professionally unemployed. They defend the salary of the medical doctor out of respect for the amount of education, high cost of that education, and deserved social status of the position. But when presented with the idea of a celebrity or CEO being worthy of their greater salaries, most stop defending the system quite so vehemently. It is as if these lower levels, that perhaps meet equitable standards, are enough to justify the horribly inequitable upper spectrum of the system. This is the part that brings the whole system to its moral demise and there is no separating the one extreme end from the rest of it. For the middle income segment, their earning power signifies their worth in society. The thought process of most middle income segment workers is that those who make less obviously need to try harder, assume the risks and hazards, and stop complaining. But when we get to the upper echelons, with some exceptions like doctors, there comes a challenge. Most people recognize that the filthy rich are not better than everyone else and their exorbitant salaries are not justified for any occupation, much less theirs. But to deny the rich their position in society jeopardizes the working segment's own position. This would eliminate whatever dreams they had of achieving a similar success. And, if you think about, it would also lessen their own feelings of superiority to those that make less than they do.

Smith later goes into depth about why teachers are so underpaid. His acknowledgment of this fact though is to say that it is advantageous for society to have access to teaching at a low cost. That is rational, if applied very narrowly. It appears that, to Smith, the fact that this entire profession is relegated to meager subsistence is trivial. There is no discussion from him regarding how future teachers could be attracted to the profession or how they might improve upon their station. He very arrogantly and dismissively declares that since there is an overabundance of educated men with no professional skill, it is well and good for the public to take advantage of this circumstance. Further, he demonstrates an attitude that those who would be teachers are not worthy of greater consideration or effort. He completely fails to acknowledge that if the profession itself is so low paying and undesirable, there is no hope of attracting people with greater skill or enthusiasm to it. He seems willing to accept that society should relegate itself to accepting cheap, unmotivated teachers with no incentive for improvement. It appears, by his estimation, appropriate for society to exploit this particular profession for its own benefit without an iota of consideration for the deplorable state in which they are left. His opinions regarding the teaching profession convey what I perceive to be a sense of disdain, with value placed only on what teachers produce or have to offer in the way of service.

The concern here is not simply the particular profession or even the state of that profession at the time of his writing the book. It is the utter absence of concern on his behalf at the forward looking consideration for the benefit of society or the people involved in his otherwise sterile assessment. His analyzation of the ramifications of this proposed economic system is centered totally upon the financial aspect. The analysis is completely amoral and the negative consequences it has on HUMAN BEINGS appears to be of no importance to him. This is exactly what Marx and Engels were talking about when they asserted that capitalism dehumanizes people and reduces their value to that of their fiscal worth. We often complain about being treated like numbers and how the human aspect has become inconsequential. Is it any wonder considering that much of what we do today is based upon this callous study done by Smith?

The MIB, the Medical Information Bureau, not the Men In Black, is a non-profit organization consisting of over 700 insurance companies. It assists the individual insurance companies in exchanging information regarding past, present, and potential clients. This free exchange of information amongst them helps the companies to individually perform more effective underwriting. So if I apply for insurance at Company A, Company A then contacts the Medical Information Bureau and gives them my information. If I filed a claim or had any health risks discovered by any of the other 700 companies, they in turn disclose that information to Company A, which uses the information to decide if they should charge me more or possibly even reject me, totally due to the risk I pose to the financial wellbeing of Company A (read: I have a greater probability of being audacious enough to actually utilize the insurance services for which I am paying). By sharing this data with each other, the insurance companies are able to efficiently determine what rates to charge each person in order to maximize their ability to profit. They realize it is beneficial for them to collude because they have a significantly higher probability of discovering any and all medical issues for each applicant. This has a huge impact on risk and profit so they are willing to forgo the free market competitive aspect. How in the world is this advantageous to consumers?

Now you can argue that this can and should be remedied with the proper regulation. Yet the first element of the vaunted free market system is that it is supposed to be self-regulated. It is supposed to balance itself naturally. Regulation is the most hated and opposed suggestion by those who purport the great benefits of free market economies. John Maynard Keynes was an economist who in the early 20th century had sweeping influence on our current economic theories. According to Smith and Keynesian theories, collusion should not take place at all because of the wondrous self-balancing nature of the free market. This though, is just another example of how, without strict regulation, the system that is supposed to be hindered by regulation will result in consumers being taken advantage of. This defies Smith's theory in every way possible. In fact, the free market theories rely heavily upon competitiveness as the source for success.

By reading Smith's own work, it is clear the main objective of capitalism is to secure the maximum amount of control and profitability for the one percent. At every juncture, Smith upholds what is advantageous to the one percent and ignores the ensuing negative impact upon the proletariats (workers) and consumers. The very foundation of capitalism, the economic system we employ and defend, is based largely upon Smith's work. How can anyone who is not a member of the one percent believe that capitalism works for the best interests of society? It is a lie. For all its promise and supposedly unique benefits, capitalism actually does very little except serve as a vehicle to ensure that the rich stay rich. This is the most important part. To be able to understand why and how those in control of wealth have convinced us of the lie that capitalism actually benefits the masses.

A common argument is that demand will outstrip supply in AISE. Apparently, without the saving grace of capitalism's genius capacity to control consumption rates through price controls, we would all consume every resource or enviable good to the point of eradication like a hoard of locusts or consume goods to the point of death. If we are so incapable of rational restraint and intellectual capacity, how can one possibly argue this same society should then be allowed to rule itself democratically? You can't win both sides of the argument. Either we are the most irrational, most inept species or society to ever exist, or we actually have the requisite cognitive function to make cogent decisions. Take your pick, but it can't be both.

The truth is that Smith actually addresses the problem of public versus private property. He does not propose that the problem lies in some supposed innate failing of human intelligence or restraint, like some mentally incompetent dog that eats dog food until it dies. In fact, the predicament only manifests itself as a direct result of the application of capitalism. This is because if you make everyone solely responsible for their own survival, they are then logically obliged to take every advantage presented to them in order to ensure the greatest probability of their survival. Therefore, when presented with a public lake where access is free, it only makes sense that one would then desire to catch every possible fish from the lake. This, of course, would be to one's greatest advantage. If one applies restraint, there is the possibility someone else would take all the fish or that too many others would fish in the same lake, making all the fish disappear in short order. In either latter scenario, that person suffers a handicap to his or her survival chances, in comparison to the first option of catching as many fish as possible. In contrast, if the lake is privately owned, the person has an incentive not to overfish as it would then be counterintuitive to eradicate the otherwise naturally replenishing resource. So in Smith's estimation, the ownership of private property serves to curtail this drive to overconsume.

In theory, if the demand for fish increases, the price for fish goes up. Suppliers want to increase the supply of fish since price and demand are high. The owner of the lake increases production levels by catching more fish and other competitors also begin catching more fish too. Eventually, supply levels increase to meet the new demand and it all balances out. How is that any different from the following scenario? The demand for fish increases. Society democratically (or as a republic) decides to increase fishing to meet the demand. If society deems further increases of fishing would be detrimental to the good of the society, then fishing is leveled out. As with all things, the fish would be equitably distributed. If one wishes to exchange the fish with someone else for something different, then they are certainly free to do so. We would simply curtail or increase resources to adapt to the current demand. Capitalism does the same thing, in a more convoluted manner, yet people celebrate the alleged intuitive nature of the system.

Capitalism seeks to control consumption through price manipulation but when survival responsibility is shared in Altruistically Inspired Societal Economics, as is the conservation of resources, there is no logical need to overconsume. If we are to believe that the private owner of the lake would logically want to ensure the longevity of the fish resource, then there is no reason why the community would not hold the same logical desire. What benefit would they have to overconsume to the point that the resource was lost? The key difference here is that in AISE, all members of the society are equitably provided for. Therefore, there is no motivation to hoard as there is when faced with being held solely accountable without an alternative recourse for survival or prosperity. Whether we apply Smith's approach that supply will create its own demand or Keynesian thought where demand drives supply, we see that both have serious proven flaws in their execution.

If one wants to point out that it is possible there will be those who are greedy and want more than their share or that there may be some who want to malinger and steal what they have not earned, I would say it is not only possible, but in fact, certain this will be true. But if a total lack of crime and abiding by the laws of a system by 100% of the population are the only acceptable standards in proving whether such a system could work, then how does one justify the use of capitalism? There is a clearly established history of stealing, embezzling, and other forms of malfeasance, but none of this is considered as proof that capitalism does not work. On the contrary, these issues are often looked upon as simply an ugly side of capitalism rather than a direct effect of it. Logically speaking, should one have a greater expectation of crimes predicated on greed and personal financial gain in a system which preaches self-preservation and dreams of vast personal wealth or in a system that upholds the ideals of survival as a community and equitable comfort for all?

Some may continue to argue that the absence of price increases to inhibit demand, and thus the ability to prevent overconsumption, will be lost. Tuna anyone? There are already similar problems today that continue unabated despite price hikes, and the overconsumption of tuna is a prime example. So this lacks any validity as a reasonable argument, as the current system irrefutably suffers from this same weakness. Didn't we wipe out the buffalo too? How is this possible when prices should have reacted to the scarcity of resources to drive down demand? It happened because killing buffalo was highly profitable and thus everyone wanted in on the profitability. The mass influx of hopeful profiteers drove an overabundance of supply which then drove prices back down. This actually increased demand and the cycle became self-perpetuating. So what was supposed to be balanced out in short order, spun wildly out of control. These are just two examples of how (again) supply and demand do not work as Smith and other economists want us to believe. What are the other repetitive characteristics of this situation? You guessed it; the one percent profits and Smith couldn't possibly care less about the detriment to the environment or people.

Capitalism is driven solely by the pursuit of profit without remorse or humanity. If you embrace this ideology without reservation, then I pity you. We have an obligation to make moral considerations an integral part of our economics, rather than its current status as an afterthought. How long will we defend a system that motivates us to self-destructively pillage our own natural resources in the quest for profit? Gluttony is a product of fear or entitlement. One fears losing or never having again so one consumes voraciously when the opportunity presents itself. Or one feels entitled to always having as much as they want and they prove it by consuming wastefully. These fears are not a product of people who work for what they get and are confident in the safety of facing obstacles communally.

Morality and Economics

Each of us has a responsibility for all humankind. It is time for us to think of other people as true brothers and sisters and to be concerned with their welfare, with lessening their suffering.

The Dalai Lama

S. Ambirajan of the Indian Institute of Technology in Madras sagely observes that happiness, ethics, and economic values are deeply interwoven, based upon extensive historical research. That while distinctly different in their own rights, the three can hardly be considered in a vacuum independent of each other. It is this very concept which I appeal to and hope that you can recognize that capitalism creates a perversion of happiness in the form of materialistic greed and leaves ethics for dead on the side of the road. If you dissent, then ask yourself why buying yourself some trinket gives you as much, if not more, joy then buying a hungry kid some food?

As to the second point, is a great society really defined by the sheer volume of its laws? With the necessity to account for every conceivable methodology one might utilize to circumvent the good of society for personal gain, as we see now in this country? I was under the belief that a great society was defined by its ability to agree to the adherence of a code of conduct in broad terms with the conviction to uphold the spirit of those principles. This is not an insinuation that we should abolish all laws, but we should strive for a state where we don't have people defending their clearly criminal acts against society due to semantics. The Sarbanes-Oxley Act of 2002 is essentially nothing more than a highly detailed and more stringent definition of accounting practices which were already in place. This will work only until the next person is caught slipping through another semantic loophole.

The problem is that we foster this behavior with our capitalist rhetoric and practices, but somehow we're still shocked by the uncaring behavior that it in turn creates. This then makes us demoralized so much that we support behavior we know to be wrong. We chuckle, grin, and high five because someone was crafty enough to find the right loophole. "Way to stick it to the man!" The problem is "the man" isn't going to pay for it in a system controlled by "the man". Instead the 99 percent of us pay for that malfeasance. Don't we realize that yet? The one percent aren't losing anything. When is the last time the one percent got penalized or funded a stimulus package? So we're cutting off our proverbial nose to spite our faces. It makes no sense.

Before determining whether happiness is achievable and to what degree, it must be determined what happiness is.

When it comes to saying of what
happiness consists, opinions differ.

Aristotle

This was Aristotle's learned observation. Is happiness in fact the collection of baubles and trinkets without consideration to the manner in which the procurement is manifested or the associated humanitarian concerns of said procurement methods? To quote Conan, the Barbarian not O'Brien, in response to the query; What is best in life?

Crush your enemies. See them
driven before you. Hear the
lamentations of their women.

Conan the Barbarian

Is this the definition of happiness? Or is happiness more in tune with Shinto ideals of harmony and peace? S. Ambirajan notes how Drakopoulos dispels common oversight when considering the hedonism of Epicurus, because at the core of his debauchery, Epicurus still held a secondary goal of peace of mind. Or is happiness to be determined as it is discussed in Book IV of the Republic? Socrates and Adeimantus, while attempting to establish their perfect city of Kallipolis, determine that it is neither practical nor possible to promote and establish equal happiness amongst all the citizens. They instead agree that it is only feasible to promote the highest possible level of satisfaction within the individuals with respect to their specific subcategory of the population. So that, according to them, a farmer may be able to achieve a level of happiness that is quite prodigious and enviable, a guardian may only be allowed to know a more stunted level of happiness. Their interpretation of what necessitates a great guardian and the lifestyle to which they must be relegated greatly influences this reasoning. Do we also believe that the level of happiness of a person should be determined by their profession? If not, explain why we then have no care that a plastic surgeon makes significantly more money than a teacher. Particularly in capitalism where money does buy happiness. Disagree? Ask someone who is getting evicted how happy they are. Ask someone who can't buy their kids birthday presents how happy they are. Ask someone who has a few days left to live, but their spouse still has to go to work each day, how happy they are.

We need to accept that capitalism and its consumption-driven dogma is destroying our souls. Almost like an alcoholic who comes to the understanding that while it may seem pleasurable and good to satisfy the desire to drink with excessive consumption, it is in fact having the opposite effect. We need to change our definition of happiness first. We need to consciously connect what we have already subconsciously realized. And that is that the catharsis we have been searching for is not going to be satisfied by consuming more. We can stop waiting and yearning for *the* trinket that will finally bring us peace, like some junkie looking for the high that will forever give them peace. Modern economics has strayed too far toward the concentration of establishing wealth and has utterly ignored ethics and happiness. So much so that we can't even figure out how to find happiness any more.

Ethics pertain more to a sociological assertion of appropriate versus inappropriate behavior in how it affects relations with our societal members. Morals have a much more theological and spiritual connotation, but essentially address the same issues in that they establish the distinctions of acceptable behavior. The biggest difference being that morals place more emphasis on the importance of the behavior for the spiritual benefit of the individual rather than the effect of the choices on society. I choose to use morals in my verbiage intentionally, as it is my unapologetic intention to write this based on a feeling of moral necessity.

However, in recognition of the tightrope I alluded to earlier, I do not wish to alienate readers based upon my moral and religious beliefs. I feel that there is still great value to what I propose in a secular viewpoint based on ethics, as well. While I am confident in my preferences and vision of happiness, it is not my intention to see the aforementioned fictitious fears of the oppression of socialism come true. So I would not and do not suggest that any particular religious set of principles needs to be set in place. Again, the great fallacy is that AISE requires dictatorial subjugation. Implementing AISE is possible, and considering the current trends regarding social behavior in this country, we could agree to adopt a policy that focused more on taking care of our fellow humans and building stronger social relations. The latter part to be accomplished in part through more time to partake in activities focused on building and providing services for and with the community.

S. Ambirajan's extensive historical research supports this statement:

The Greek philosophers were quite clear about the existence of good, right, just and virtuous pleasures and those that were not. They believed that the individual's happiness achieved by any means whatsoever was not acceptable if it failed to ensure social happiness.

S. Ambirajan

We all recognize that there are finite resources. Logically then, we must concede that in order for me to be exceedingly rich, there must be those who are proportionately poor. It is conceptually impossible in capitalism to increase one's wealth without negatively impacting someone else's, because it is unavoidable when inequitably distributing a finite amount of resources. This is exacerbated on a geometric scale when the inequity achieves the level we see in current capitalism. So how then do we continue to justify our own decline in this matter of moral behavior? How then do we call ourselves superior? I don't know about you, but fancier gadgets and absent moral direction, do not define a superior society to me.

If the cure for cancer is discovered tomorrow, do you really think that it will be given to everyone who needs it? Or is it going to be given to those who can *afford* it? Almost 40% of all people will be diagnosed with cancer at some point in their lives and 44 million Americans are still without health insurance. Do you think the unfortunate ones who fall into both categories will be able to afford this new cure? Why are the children of celebrities able to go to private schools, eat nothing but the highest quality food, and receive healthcare from the best physicians, while the children of a janitor go to underfunded public schools, may need food stamps to have enough to eat, and are lucky if they have healthcare of any kind? Aren't we saying that the celebrity kids are worth more than the janitor's kids? They deserve a better life because of who their parents are? I am no expert in theology, but I am unaware of any major religion that teaches: If one should offer goods/services of value then certainly treat them with respect and consideration, but otherwise treat them like dirt and with indifference to their needs or suffering. Think about that, because that is the core of capitalism and yet any religion and even most generally accepted standards of decorum teach something totally in defiance of this callous attitude. Don't most social practices and religions teach that we should be giving, caring, and compassionate and further don't they typically specify this ideal with regard to strangers or those in need? This is logical as it is assumed that one would already take care of family, friends, and those whose wellbeing is linked to himself/herself.

While we have done away with terms like aristocracy and titles such as Baron and Duke to denote the worth of a person, we have simply replaced them with terms like politicians and titles such as CEO and CFO to denote the worth of a person. Instead of a family name being worthy of instant worth classification, now it is by occupation. So instead of someone whispering "He's a Schtuppenhieger" to impress people as to that person's worth, now it is "He's a lawyer". Is the Ranger's life worth less than the Green Beret's, because he has less training or is a lower rank? Is the plumber's life worth less than a civil engineer? If you want to argue that treating all human life equally is too idealistic, then do you honestly believe that the lives of football players, CEO's, and movie stars are really worth more than the lives of school teachers and bus drivers?

Well if that is not the case then why are we allowing some people to live a life where not just luxuries, but certain basic amenities, are made unavailable to them? How can you say that we are not establishing a hierarchy of human worth? How is this different from segregation? Why don't we tell a class of students, those whose parents make more than $100,000 will be taught a different curriculum than those whose parents do not? All of these are examples of providing specific groups of people with goods and services of greater value by arbitrary determination. This is why all students are supposed to be taught the same thing- regardless of race, creed, religion, or income. Really, if we are not placing a financial value on people's lives then explain how it is okay for a multimillion dollar celebrity who has HIV being able to slap down cash in order to get the medications they need to live; while a dental hygienist needs to mortgage everything and go into debt in order to get those same meds and still be able to eat or have electricity. How is this not telling one person that their life is not worth as much as the other? There is no shortage of medication. We just will not give it to you because you have not "earned" it.

Yes some people are stronger, smarter, faster, or more talented than others. There is no denying that. But that should not determine that any one person's life is more valuable than another person's life. These unique attributes should be appreciated and celebrated, but not as a measuring stick for the level of comfort they are entitled to above those not as pretty, as smart, or as fast. We look upon the caste system in India with arrogant contempt, but how are we any different when we pay a model millions of dollars because she is pretty and let a guy struggle because "all he can do" is fix a car engine? How is this not placing a monetary value on someone's life? How is this not arbitrary and unsympathetic? Does that make him less of a father or a human being because he is not a supermodel too? I don't care if you're the most ingenious person on the planet, are you really telling me that you have greater entitlement to comfort than someone who has an I.Q. of 46? Why? Because you are better at marketing strategies than the other person? How is it, that this makes sense to us? The fact that someone can hit a 100 mile per hour fastball on a somewhat regular basis means that they deserve to live in lavishness? Is it clear that a person born with cerebral palsy should be content with a less lucrative career since they are certainly not as "productive" as the baseball player? Success is just as accessible to the other person if they just persevere as much as the baseball player did, right? How does any of this satisfy any sense of morality on any scale? Yet this is capitalism.

The only thing that justifies this is the sense of balance and "earning it" that capitalism pushes. The one percent have *earned* the right to enjoy themselves and to *choose* where their money goes and if they want to have a lavish party it is their *right*. And within this morally desolate economic system we engage in, all those conventions are absolutely correct. That's not my point. My point is that when you recognize that the system is spiritually devoid and that we should be viewing this in a humanitarian context instead, then all of those conventions are utterly wrong. We judge right and wrong based on the production of wealth and profit. These rich people are good at jobs that happen to generate high volumes of wealth so they have *earned* it, can *choose* what to do with it, and have the *right* to this. Now look at it from a humanitarian perspective. Has the family of the 12 year old girl who is dying of leukemia *earned* the ridiculous medical bills; did they *choose* to have this happen; what *rights* do they have? Shouldn't we be living by the conventions that, we *choose* to live in a society where everyone *earns*, through honest effort, the *right* to an equitably comfortable existence? We are not God and it is not our place to try to make this Heaven on Earth. I believe that it is our place and our charge from God to do what we are capable of, to make this world better and to care for each other to the best of our ability. Even if you don't believe in God, doesn't this still sound like a more worthy goal than, make as much money as you can before you die?

Hypothetically: Your kid is complaining of hunger pains and you just finish stuffing your face to the point that you just can't bear to take another bite. It is not until this point that you magnanimously offer the last few morsels of food to your child to eat. This does not make you a good parent. I would hope that all of you would agree with this. How then does one think that securing great personal wealth and security for ourselves first and then rationing out charitable contributions of the superfluous funds is any better? Even if the amounts of those portions of superfluous funds is enormous. The most revered donor of charity in the Bible is the woman who gives a mere $.02. Why? Because it was everything she had. But if we all give all that we have, then we are all secure. There is no need for charity.

Now some people will say that the difference here is that in the former example it is a family member that is being taken care of and the latter is referring to people who are not family. Are those the only two categories that truly matter? So after thousands of years of human evolution and social progression are we going to continue to cling to an antiquated and simplistic categorization of the human race by family sur names? This country loves its associations. People proudly displaying T-shirts, bumper stickers, flags, and hats emblazoned with the affiliation of which they are most proud of being part of. Whether it be America, a particular state, university, organization, or some other entity. Well this is what I'm talking about. We can't just continue to hovel together in our separate homes and guard, protect, and provide for our separate little family units. We have a responsibility to each other. We are tied together in the simple fact that we are a society. The survival, choices, and wellbeing of each individual affects all the other members of the society.

Instead of reveling in and relying on grandiose and heartwarming charitable moments, it should be a part of who we are every day. Didn't we all do better when our parents demonstrated their love for us each day? Isn't that what we longed for? Isn't that what we strive for as parents? No kid wants their mom and dad to only show them affection and support a couple days out of the year, randomly, or worse just around Christmas time. How do marriages end? Because we get into a rut and instead of being the norm, affection becomes a rarely celebrated moment. The glory and lingering positivity of that affection can be enough to sustain happiness for a while. Until those moments become so far in between that the glimmer fades as soon as the moment ends. Eventually the relationship dies because it can no longer tolerate the prolonged periods of desolation. Let's stop being charitable and let's start making this part of our daily lives. Let's not make lavish events of these random examples of charity, but instead make the choice to care about people every day.

While I myself point out the discrepancies of other cultures and policies, it is for the sake of demonstrating how further change was needed and eventually happened. That the existence of these discrepancies is not justification for disregarding the value of previous progress, but the acknowledgement that at least progress was being made. While it is easy to ridicule and judge what we can now see from our perspective, which were continuing issues that would need to be rectified later, it is far more difficult to recognize those same issues in our current time. It is even harder to have the courage and conviction necessary to rectify said issues. Just as we do not insinuate that the lessons learned from building the first car or plane should be disregarded because we have learned so much since then, neither should we have the same approach when considering social evolution. We have built upon each new discovery made in automotive engineering and aeronautics to achieve what we have today. We continue to do so in fact. So why should we not apply this same rationale to that of the development of our social beliefs? Instead of judging those in the past, perhaps we ought to build upon what they began, to build something better.

It is no longer tolerable to only allow those of specific heritage, title, race, or sex to pursue the accumulation of wealth. We currently accept that we can stand equally opposed in the pursuit of wealth. This is progress and should not be discounted. 100 years ago women would not even be considered for certain employment. 200 years ago even the few free African Americans were not that free. Women, Caucasians, Jews, Latinos, conservatives, and gays stand unopposed and on equal footing. So now all are allotted fair chance to gain and keep wealth rather than being denied such freedom, but we should not be content to lay stagnant here though. Capitalism necessitates the existence of "haves" and "have nots", so as one person gains opportunity so too does another lose said opportunity. Instead of standing in equal opposition to one another in the pursuit of wealth, why not stand as equals in the sharing of that wealth?

Human Nature?

*Be the change that you wish to see
in the world.*

Mahatma Gandhi

A common defense against altruistic principles is that there are already well established lazy segments of our society both in the form of the super rich and the super poor. We create lazy and entitled people and then lament the failings of "human nature" and use this as a justification for why AISE could never possibly work. Laziness is not a natural problem, it is a conditioned problem. Even animals in a zoo become lazy. It has been proven in tests, that once animals have been conditioned to receive food from simply pressing a button, they become too lazy to try to get food any other way. The solution does not require complex mathematics. You simply remove the factors that enable and condition people to be lazy and self-entitled. That is not to say that reconditioning is simple or instantaneous. It must be done properly and over time. This certainly seems to be a better alternative to continuing the poor practice of conditioning and enabling people to be lazy though.

Another common argument is that greed is not just a strong element of human nature, but actually the overwhelming drive. This misplaced idea is justification for the argument that greed needs to be satiated and therefore AISE is impossible. The following is a statement by B.B. Price, a Professor of Ancient and Medieval History at York University, Toronto, Canada, and a visiting Professor at Massachusetts Institute of Technology:

Ambirajan observes that across all ancient cultures, hedonistic advocates in search of extreme forms of pleasure appear to have been relatively few, and selfishness is presented as the confusion of body for true Self.

B.B. Price

From a historical context we see little evidence to support such a claim of greed being an uncontrollable element in sociological issues. Likely this is due to the fact that we share a similarity with other social animals. Of course our intellect has an effect on this, but it is undeniable that social animals recognize the need to maintain the integrity of the group. While the alpha male will take the lion's share to ensure his own survival, it is still understood that the strength of the pack is essential for the survival of all. This holds greater meaning for human society thousands of years ago when one person could not possibly provide all the needs for survival by themselves. One person could not possibly hunt, farm, collect wood, ensure safety, make clothing, and all the other necessities.

Today we can afford to be less considerate to each other on a daily basis, because technology both simplifies processes so as to not need the effort of so many and allows longer intervals between interactions. I don't need to see a cobbler, get help thatching my roof, or shoe my horse regularly. A pair of shoes lasts a year, I can go a few years before I need to have house repairs, my car goes 6 months between oil changes, and a refrigerator and canned goods mean I'm not dependent on daily interactions with the grocer. While we still definitely need each other, modern technology has helped create a false sense of independence. It is false because when it is time to buy a pair of shoes, I have no idea how to make them myself so I need the skills of the shoemakers. I am a good farmer, but I do not have the time to grow everything I need. We falsely believe that we are not as dependent on the strength of society, because we can go for long periods between moments of necessity. This misconception allows us to ignore the importance of maintaining the strength of the society and thus allows us to indulge our feelings of greed more freely. The reality is that we are actually so specialized today that we are more dependent upon each other than ever before. Can you set a bone, grow your own food, vaccinate your dog, fix your car engine, make your own clothes, and file your own taxes?

Further, while greed is in fact identified as one of the seven deadly sins, it is still only one of seven deadly sins. If AISE is impossible because of greed, then by consistent application of logic, capitalism should be impossible due to the existence of envy. Because it should be the goal of everyone to have what everyone else has, creating a state of constant chaos and upheaval as everyone connives, rapes, steals, and murders to possess that which they envy in an economic system predicated on "haves" and "have nots". This is a society that still places a great deal of respect and importance in the sanctity of marriage. Sure there are some other legal considerations too, but why such the fervor to extend the right of marriage to homosexuals if it holds no importance? So how can this society still look with favor upon the institution of marriage when lust exists? Shouldn't lust make marriage an impossibility?

The seven deadly sins are indeed powerful in their temptation and are highly prevalent, but they are not universal. They should not be the cause to cease making the effort to uphold moral behavior. They are not presented as an excuse for bad behavior. They are not discussed with the philosophy of "with the existence of these, why shouldn't we sin?" Like a teenager having the epiphany that having a party should be a given, due to the fact that his parents are gone for the weekend. The purpose of defining and discussing the seven deadly sins is to create awareness of them and the need to consciously guard against their negative effects. In other words, realizing that greed exists and that it can influence people to do severe wrong should motivate us to reject an economic system that so blatantly celebrates greed. So the existence of greed should actually be the very reason for adopting AISE and not an argument against it.

Another misconception is that survival of the individual is the strongest natural drive and therefore selfishness will always trump altruism. Throughout the animal kingdom it can be observed that individual survival is not the greatest natural instinct. Propagation of the species is actually a much stronger drive. Sure one can look at the father bear or lion that eats the cubs and say this contradicts that. Yet that is often the drive for propagation of the species. In most cases the adult male, is typically driven by hunger or the fact that those cubs were sired by a male of inferior genetic makeup. Either way, by killing the cubs the male is attempting to ensure the survival of the genetically superior members of the species. By killing the cubs he removes the inferior genes from the gene pool or increases his own chance of survival, and thus his superior genes, by staving off hunger and creating less mouths to feed. When you look at salmon, octopi, redback spiders, squid, praying mantis, bees, and a number of marsupial species they all ignore personal survival in favor of propagation and childbirth in order to ensure the survival of the species. These are a few examples of semelparous animals, or animals that reproduce only once and then die. This does not even consider the additional list of iteroparous animals that risk their wellbeing in order to reproduce each mating season. Look at penguins that subject themselves to arduous and life threatening conditions, with the sole intent of making sure that a new generation will be born.

Then look at humans. We choose to abandon, molest, abort, and sell our kids as sex slaves. Are greed and personal survival really overriding natural instincts? Or are they justifications to deny that AISE is in fact morally superior and what we should be aspiring to? Are they merely convenient excuses so we can continue to slothfully revel in our own sinful nature? This is what the discussion of the seven deadly sins is about. The recognition that they exist and our obligation to rise above them as best we can. There is very little that is "natural" in our behavior anymore. We have been conditioned to accept certain social conventions at very early ages. Isn't that the very crux of the body image and race issues that are so prevalent today? That we teach kids from an early age, racial stigmas and the definition of physical beauty. Big boobs, blonde hair, and thin waist right? We currently acknowledge this negative conditioning effect and that is why there is a growing movement to alter our perceptions of body image. We need to differentiate between nature and conditioned responses.

People have great difficulty not only seeing things from multiple perspectives but also mistakenly assert what they see regularly in their daily lives, on everything everywhere. The term "human nature" gets thrown around a lot. Because I see the majority of people regularly act or react in a specified manner, then it must be "natural" for all humans everywhere to react similarly. It must be due to human nature. The problem with this assumption is that as "widespread" as most people believe their subject population to be, it is actually very limited.

Don't we constantly acknowledge that the world gets smaller every day? Between the internet, global social media, international trade, and the convenience of air travel today there are few isolated cultures any more. The effective expansion of American culture and capitalism has served to create shared interests and merged cultural differences. This is good and helps to unify people everywhere. In our house we eat Italian, Thai, Greek, Japanese, Chinese, American, and Mexican cuisine regularly, because of globalization. We become more aware of the concerns and habits of other cultures through documentaries and interactions with travelers. As we see the cultural lines begin to blur, it becomes too easy to misconstrue these commonalities as human nature, rather than the expansion and amalgamation of conditioned responses across cultural boundaries.

The fact that salsa is the most popular condiment in the U.S. is not proof that there is some natural predilection amongst North American people to consume spicy tomato based products. As ubiquitous as the practice is, there is no natural penchant for men to be more attracted to women who shave their legs and armpits. It is simply a widely accepted and practiced behavior that has become such a learned and conditioned response that one could easily make that conclusion. We are social creatures of habit. We are easily conditioned. We begin to become conditioned practically from the moment of birth. It is all but impossible to discern what is natural versus what is conditioned because of this. Many studies confirm the development of babies based on conditioning- whether they are cuddled, skin to skin contact, different types of visual and audio stimulus, etc. Blaming our preconceived shortcomings on "human nature" is just a lazy way to avoid responsibility and the potential effort of rectifying the shortcoming. Or is that just human nature?

We are inundated with images, actions, and behaviors in movies and television. We tend to forget that even the most realistic plotlines and writing, is all carefully crafted and designed to either elicit specific emotional responses or establish a series of events that are necessary for future plotline developments. For instance, it is pretty boring if the police meticulously plan and coordinate a breach, and thus minimize the ability of the criminals to react violently or escape. Of course in real life mistakes are made, but the vast majority of police incursions are done like this and with zero incident. Yet we regularly see in movies and on T.V. where the breach is made and then there is a prolonged and exciting gun fight and chase. My favorite is the backdoor that is inexplicably not covered and the bad guys have nothing to do but run through it and jump in the car that also has the keys in it. It is such a common occurrence in entertainment media that it is difficult to not think that the police are morons. The reality is that such matters are predominantly handled in a professional and effective manner, but one would never guess that from movies or T.V.

Many arguments are made both in general society and the psychology community, about how we are affected by conditioning and the desire to conform. There are business formulas and computer programs designed to predict human flocking in order to better gauge consumer patterns. Marketing is all about influencing, instilling, and sparking the desire to consume based on what is popular. The use of politically correct language assists in subtly conditioning us to seeing and accepting things in a new light. Most professions have their own rules of decorum. One is expected to adhere to the particular behaviors, dress codes, and attitudes that are common for that subset. Is it human nature that men do not wear skirts? That is a common trend across many cultures, so shouldn't that strengthen the argument? At best, one could argue that greed and selfishness are unavoidable. In that the general populace is simply conforming to the conditioned traits commonly fostered in the practice of capitalism. So converting to AISE then should actually be quite simple using the argument of human nature. Because as the new cultural standard becomes altruistically considering the societal impact of economics then people should *naturally* seek to conform to this new standard, just as they did to the greed and selfishness supported by capitalism.

The Dichotomy of Our Society

*We make a living by what we get,
but we make a life by what we
give.*

Winston Churchill

The most puzzling problem with capitalism, is the dichotomous attitude we have toward it. We laud people for their aggressive financial success, but we also complain about the ensuing fiscal inequality. We openly acknowledge the moral depravity that such success inherently necessitates, but then we're surprised at how inconsiderate employers are to our needs. "Driving a hard bargain" is great if you are the recipient of the benefits of said bargain, but most of us at one point or another find ourselves on the other side of that hard bargain. It is only at that time that the commendable aspects suddenly become problems with the system that need correcting due to their lack of fairness.

It has been rumored that an executive for the South Korean division of the pharmaceutical company Roche said:

*We are not in the business to save
lives, but to make money. Saving
lives is not our business.*

Alleged Unknown

Supposedly this was in response to criticism for Roche refusing to lower their prices for a year's supply of an HIV medication called Fuzeon, from $25,000 to $18,000. Even at $18,000, it was still highly profitable. This statement could and possibly should be the very mantra of capitalism. Yet, inexplicably, many ardent supporters of capitalism were highly critical of this alleged statement and also for the act of refusing to sell the medication in South Korea at the requested lower price. From a purely academic view how is this not the very embodiment of capitalism? What about this statement is untrue, in those terms? Nothing. We abhor the actions of Martin Shkreli. I'm not talking about anything else except for his act of purchasing the exclusive rights to sell an important drug for treating complications associated with HIV and then deciding to dramatically increase the price from $13.50 per pill to $750.00 per pill. This is capitalism. This is not an unwanted side effect. It is not the ugly side. It *is* capitalism. The price is determined at the discretion of the controller of the good or service and that is supposed to be for the most profit that demand will support. Our supposed influence on this is the option to not purchase the goods. Period.

There is a supply curve and a demand curve. Where they meet is where the price is theoretically supposed to be established. There is no third "humanitarian considerations" curve that is supposed to affect pricing. We celebrate all the great benefits that capitalism supposedly creates, but we cringe at and deny the ugly truth of its effects. This is like cheering on a person who beats people into a coma and then later yelling at that person for being a heartless monster. Capitalism exploits people coming and going; by "maximizing their value" which means working them as much as possible for as little compensation as possible and then "maximizing profits" which means squeezing out as much as possible from them in price. Then we're baffled when people have nothing to show in terms of money at the end of the day. We support an economic system that encourages people to be greedy. We believe we should make as much money as we can, raise stock value through the roof, and not give free handouts. But then we say, "For goodness sake don't charge *too* much." The irreconcilable difference between what we demand in adherence to our economic system and what we know to be right in our souls is dizzying.

Many like to use the arguments of "well that's just one version of capitalism", "that's just extreme capitalism", "capitalism doesn't have to be that way". These are lies people tell themselves. It is analogous to saying that a vegetarian who refuses to eat meat is just "practicing extreme vegetarianism". Or "vegetarianism doesn't have to be that way". That *is* vegetarianism. There is no getting around that. There are no provisions in capitalism for cutting prices for humanitarian reasons. The only driving factors in capitalism are supply and demand. Even if they had agreed to the price of $18,000, is that really much better? Do you think that you would be more appreciative of the lower price if you only had $2,000? Ask yourself what an appropriate price should be. If $25,000 is just "extreme capitalism" then what is "acceptable capitalism"? I guarantee the definition of "acceptable capitalism" will differ between someone making $150,000 a year and someone making $28,000 a year. I dare you to defend the need for profitability, the complexity of research and development costs, and the importance of shareholder value to someone who has contracted hepatitis B, has no insurance, and $500. I can't. I can no longer look at our economic system and defend profitability over life or needless suffering.

I understand and in fact have made the same ignorant argument myself about the need to charge so much for medications because of the high cost and risk associated with research. It is absolutely true that the cost of research is very expensive and there is a long and costly process to performing clinical trials which then leads to a long and costly approval process. There is also no guarantee that any of this expenditure, time, and effort will result in any income. A tremendous amount of risk is associated with investing all of these resources and potentially procuring nothing. Then one needs to consider the need to be profitable. Now it is not even just enough to recoup the original value of the resources invested into the process, but now all that needs to be multiplied in order to create a profit margin large enough to warrant such risk in the first place. Calculations are used in business in order to account for inflationary and interest earning considerations during this period of R&D, which serves to raise the required level of profitability even higher. In understanding all this, it becomes clearly evident that these high prices are not only justified, but necessary. There is no alternative, but to sacrifice those who lack the financial means to afford it. Does this really sound right to you?

This is all true *if* we fail to see that there is one simple solution to all of this. The alternative is to have the courage to see that we can alter this concrete reality and make something completely new by removing one aspect of the whole scenario. Profit. If we remove the need and desire to create this manmade construct known as profit, suddenly there is zero reason for not providing everyone with what they *need*. Remember two things here. We're not talking about unlimited lip balm, we're talking about life saving medications. Second, profit is a manmade idea that is not necessary. Profit is what we think it is. Ergo if we want to change how our system functions, we just need to redefine what profit means to us. We need to say that we no longer want profit that creates immeasurable luxury for the one percent, but that profit should be the proliferation of enough goods to satisfy the needs of as many as is possible, given the restrictions of time and resources. This definition is not perfect, but it is real and it is moral. It is also conceivable.

For those who don't believe that altering our economic system is possible and more than that, realistic, consider the highly speculative nature of our current system. All the Federal Reserve needs to do is use innuendo in a press release to create real change in the value of the stock market and drive or stagnate purchasing. The mere mention of a hike of the interest rates can have very real consequences. Hiring and firing decisions are influenced by these statements and choices regarding the interest rates. Prices and salaries rise and fall based on these expectations as much as they do on concrete mathematically produced financial numbers. How can one possibly say that we cannot choose to redefine the value of a good or service, when in fact our whole system is predicated upon doing exactly that? How is it that a CD can sell for $26 and five years later the exact same, still sealed, CD can sell for $2? How can a stock price plummet for no other reason than the fact that a big group of people choose to sell it off at the same time? It is all predicated upon expectations, faith, and our created definitions.

That is why we have the problems we currently do. We are so caught up in the contraptions of our creations that we forget that is exactly what they are- contraptions of our own creation. We artificially manipulate prices and create inflation, because the whole system is arbitrary and is totally reliant on faith. That's right, capitalism is an economic system based on people *believing* it will work. In fact it is people's fluctuating lack of faith or increased confidence that actually causes prices and values to ebb and flow. The surgeon and the operating room only cost $10,000, because we say they do. In order to fit into our current system, we need to assign them a cost and it must fit within our expectations. Why does the same hamburger cost $3 in America and 338.67 yen in Japan? Is this because they are a lot hungrier for hamburgers? Are they starving over there? Do they just like carrying around large denomination bills? No, it is because the monetary value is arbitrary and it can fluctuate greatly depending on the machinations of the one percent and a society's expectations.

When we dispense with the exchange system and simply provide based on our ability and the resource levels, things change drastically. That is not to foolishly believe that Utopia will ensue. There will be limitations, but they will not be falsely generated ones due to the rich hoarding resources for themselves. The new limitations will be real. They will be based on the reasonable work schedule of the workers and the availability of the resources and facilities. There will still need to be order in how it is determined that people receive goods or services.

Before capitalism the conventional thought process was that squeezing the populace for as much labor and tax as possible was the path to amassing the greatest level of wealth possible. Stimulating thought and ingenuity is counterintuitive to this process, so these were actively stifled. The bourgeoisie that adopted capitalism realized that by rewarding the working class slightly more, enough to feed the dream, the one percent actually realized greater levels of wealth. The dangling carrot stimulated the masses to work harder and be more productive than ever before. The modern "emerging leadership" paradigms that espouse ethics, morality, and community are just more rhetoric to satisfy the current dissatisfaction. Essentially it is a new form of mind control for the masses by preaching a sensitive, philosophical refrain that makes no coherent sense and has even less proof of practical application. More often than not, the underlying driving forces behind these heartwarming mantras is that of greater public approval, ergo greater consumer loyalty, ergo higher profit margins. Higher profit margins as the de facto motivating factor? What a surprise. While we tell ourselves that capitalism has climbed to this higher mountain of philosophical responsibility and morality, really it just took a new path to end up at the same spot. A more picturesque and slightly more fulfilling path, but it still ends up with profit being at the core of its framework.

As a society we indignantly and self-righteously condemn the behavior exhibited by Roche and Shkreli, but simultaneously defend the same selfish and unsympathetic behavior by supporting capitalism and all its social inequality. It's a clear double standard. We forget that we see what we have created. The greed, egotism, and immorality that we see is a byproduct of the very economic system that we defend. We laud and magnify greed and wealth accumulation. We criticize and belittle failure to maintain specific levels of income and self-sufficiency, but then incredulously we simultaneously chastise those who do everything they can to achieve "too much" wealth.

At least we still recognize the lack of moral fortitude that such actions represent, but how much longer will we? At what point will we become so disillusioned by this nonsensical double standard that we will lose all ability to see reality for what it is? We denounce such blatant demonstrations of moral absence but immediately defend our *right* to comfort, luxury, and sometimes gluttony at the cost of other people's well-being. Of course it becomes a game of relativity, with only the highest echelons getting zero empathy or support. Few rational people will come to the defense of the politician who insists that a $170,000 annual salary is too meager for proper subsistence. Or the whining celebrity that justifies their opulent lifestyle either by claiming that their talent commands that reward or that their fragile nature necessitates it. Typically those who defend otherwise indefensible claims such as these, are those who have similar ambitions or even just empty fantasies of experiencing such inequitable lifestyles themselves.

I acknowledge that in this country there does currently exist a policy which justifies the middle income segment's view of having earned their level of comfort and personal wealth. It has been the normal practice for some time, to allow the rich to protect their wealth while forcing the hardest working segment to fund programs that provide fully for a segment that does nothing but consume handouts. I am not referring to the sick or legitimately disabled. I am not referring to those who honestly work, but need assistance. I am referring to the segment that lives off the "social" programs funded almost exclusively by the efforts of the middle income segment, while returning nothing to society. Ironically the middle income segment, which funds a large portion of these "social" programs, is then denied use of these same programs because...they make too much. This makes these "social" programs not very socialized. This obviously inequitable exchange, understandably cultivates feelings of animosity. A desire to cling to what one has justifiably earned in the current economic structure is understandable. For now I am not referring to these circumstances or the feelings which they produce. Although it should also be noted that this feeling of animosity is desired by the one percent, because it serves to create another schism between elements of the 99%.

I am referring to the defense of luxury by making excuses that one does not have nearly as much as some others. It starts with the relative statement that the more comfortable middle income segment person doesn't have a personal jet or a 50,000 square foot home on a compound. As if just because one person has more opulence than me, that I'm better. Believe me I have made the same self-serving excuses and justifications to myself. It's easy to justify the sinful nature by pointing to the "more sinful" person. It's a deplorable excuse that I am guilty of myself. It's time for all of us to accept our own responsibility for our own actions and choices. What is inequitable is inequitable, no matter the depth of it and certainly no matter the depth of someone else's. Your wrong does not justify my wrong. It is true that it is difficult for the typical middle income earner to achieve and then secure a comfortable existence. Injury, illness, or breakdown of certain high cost possessions (car, A/C unit, refrigerator, etc.) can quickly evaporate any cushion. To the person who can't afford to eat one nutritious meal a day, the ownership of quartz countertops is as lavish to him as the jet plane is to the middle income person. It is easy to get lost in the relative comparisons, unless you happen to be broke.

Take the comparison of a computer technician who earns significantly more than the waste management employee who empties trash cans. There are numerous arguments that can be made to justify one making a higher salary than the other. Some of these are: higher drive for success, greater mental capacity or learning ability, higher social importance, exclusivity of a particular talent, etc. There are also many assumptions. Lower motivation for success is not a de facto characteristic of being a waste management employee, although many would make this presumptuous argument. There are a myriad of reasons that one person is emptying trash cans for a living and the other is a computer programmer. Many of these are issues of pure circumstance and not anything to do with moral fiber or character flaws. Yet for the most part we are content to dismissively attribute certain negative, or at best inferior, attributes to the profession and ignore the human being. We base the income level, ergo a person's comfort level, for each position based on arbitrary assumptions. The person's individual value and worth as a human being is conveniently sanitized from the calculation.

There may be substance to some of these arguments, perhaps the computer technician does in fact have a higher I.Q. than the waste management employee. But does that make him a better human being? Does it truly make him more deserving of a more luxurious lifestyle? I have met highly intelligent individuals whom I greatly respect and others whom I found to be utterly reprehensible. The same goes for those of lesser intelligence. Although our economic structure may not totally ignore one's moral worth in determining financial success, it certainly is not a major factor. We reward people based on occupation rather than moral fiber. Then we wonder in amazement why we have people in the highest financially rewarding occupations who lack any understanding of social responsibility. Certainly there are exceptions to every rule, but this an applicable generalization. We know that if someone did not pick up the garbage or staff the gas station, that our society would have major issues operating correctly. We know these are necessary occupations, but then we look down upon these people, because that is *all* they do. That makes no sense. We need someone to do this, but then we belittle them for doing it.

By this virtue, if you want to consider me to be of less value because all I do is clean bathrooms, perhaps we should eliminate the occupation. Let everyone be responsible for cleaning the bathrooms at hotels, gas stations, offices, etc. If we all know the humility of the task and as we share in it, we could appreciate the value that we all have. If it is such a degrading task that it is beneath you to do, then why would you support someone else being relegated to the task? Is it because you do in fact believe that you are more worthy than them or of higher worth? We need to stop spewing popular rhetoric of equality and actually practice it. This starts by ceasing to look down upon others for holding occupations that we have decided are demeaning and yet as a society have created because we know these tasks must be fulfilled. Is it any less arbitrary to judge a human by the color of their skin than it is to judge them for their financial worth or their occupation? But we do it daily. We segregate ourselves based on materialistic value rather than spiritual value.

These are preconceived notions that we create. When you eliminate such barriers, the differences magically disappear. When 80,000 Broncos fans are cheering, there are no divisions between executive assistants, grounds keepers, or retail clerks. There is no such segregation at a Star Wars convention. Suddenly these are all just people with a common fervor for something. These people value each other as people and no one is concerned with anyone else's occupation or financial earning value. These people get together and they can communicate and relate with ease. It's only when we get back to the office or job that we must once again resign ourselves to these self-imposed categories of worth. We're all people with good and bad traits, but we're people.

Many workers take great pride in their work and effort and they understandably defend the status quo because they feel that the sacrifices that they make and risks that they assume, justify their position in the economic pecking order. This is particularly true when they think about those who allegedly make a conscious choice to work in professions that pay less. This mindset deals with the long-held adage in this country that if you want to make more, you need to be willing to sacrifice or risk more. Period. As simple as that. Those who have better jobs deserve to eat better, go on nicer vacations, and buy their kids fancier toys and luxury items than those who have lesser paying jobs. Most will also support the higher compensation of doctors, out of consideration for their extended educational commitment and the obvious benefit to everyone. Many people willingly accept that the doctor deserves the elevated luxuries the same as the typical worker does over lower level workers. So, up to this point, it is generally accepted that the financial earnings pecking order is good and just.

If the worker "earns" his/her level of comfort above those who choose to earn less by risking/sacrificing less, then this proves the correctness of the current system. Doctors who must complete the exceptional amount of learning necessary for their profession also earn their higher levels of compensation. So by this pattern of logic, the law degree holding CEO has likewise earned the higher luxury standards. Right? I mean if you wanted to earn obscene levels of pay like the typical CEO then all you need to do is go to law school or get a high level business degree too. And if you can't or choose not to, then that is your problem. Just like it's the waste management worker's choice. Right? The same holds true for politicians, right? They got a degree and got elected, so according to the way the system operates they have clearly "earned" their elevated luxury status.

This is the point at which many people balk at the fairness of compensation. The argument is that if you want to be better off, get a better job, but capitalism is designed with higher and lower paying jobs. The "menial" jobs versus the "skilled" ones. It is important to recognize that working at McDonald's is not designed as a career job and that attempting to manipulate salaries to alter this in our current system is futile. I used to buy into this interpretation that it is an entry level job and thus it is okay that it pays less. The problem is when you stop to take notice and realize that real progression is not available for everyone. We must recognize that this position is not just a stepping stone for some people. For some there is no means for progression and this is intentional. Remember that capitalism deliberately ensures that some people will not be able to adequately provide for themselves. It must, because if everyone actually could be equally successful then it would be called...AISE. There must be poor paying jobs that people have no other choice but to fill.

We do not just judge based on intelligence either. Do we not choose to wildly compensate those for their ability to slam dunk, throw a football, or hit a small white ball into a hole? The same holds true for singing a song and acting. Granted, in these professions there is a drastic difference in rates of compensation so it is not as indiscriminate as more mundane professions. The lowest rated NFL quarterback still makes quite a lot of money, but there is a significant difference between his salary and the top tier quarterback. This difference is drastically different, even percentage-wise, than most other professions. The point though is that the focus of a human's worth is based on some physical attribute or another. We financially reward, ergo provide greater means and luxury, to people based on their physical attributes.

Clearly the old adage of "it's what is on the inside that matters" is a lie. As long as one is smart and designs a useful invention, one is worth elevating and supporting. Even though someone may be morally disgraceful, we will shower that person with the ability to live lavishly. While simultaneously another person will be allowed to wallow in poverty and obscurity, because they have nothing to offer society...except for being a genuinely kind, caring, and considerate human being. Why should we care about this latter person though? They have not provided us with a next generation app that provides hours of mindless entertainment after all. They did not win the World Series. They are not great at exploiting loopholes in the legal system to allow guilty criminals to avoid being held accountable.

We have been taught that capitalism is great and wonderful. That it is not only highly beneficial, but actually totally responsible for everything that we have to be grateful for. We also see that there is a massive amount of suffering and inequality though. But because we have been so effectively brainwashed, it is inconceivable to us that capitalism itself could possibly be the reason for this suffering and inequality. So we continually look for other reasons that are not there. We ignore this clearly dichotomous attitude that we have with capitalism.

Our hearts and souls know the truth, but our brains continue to resist and seek this other reason that must be out there. We need to stop looking at this suffering and inequality through the lens of capitalism, because that is the only way this suffering and inequality makes sense. Once you ignore the explanations and justifications created by capitalism, we realize that this suffering and inequality is unnecessary and preventable.

How Capitalism Fails

Beware of false knowledge; it is
more dangerous than ignorance...

George Bernard Shaw

Modern capitalism is only about 250 years old, but there is a repetitive cycle where the government needs to break up monopolies because they get so far out of hand. There are oligopolies and monopolies throughout our current system and historically monopolies like Rockefeller, AT&T, Microsoft, and others keep getting bigger and more powerful. The recent proliferation of oligopolies and monopolies is staggering. There are now only four airlines which provide domestic air travel and even then each of them basically has a monopoly in their own specific markets. Not surprisingly, despite their claims of the opposite, since this has transpired airlines have been experiencing record profit margins. This was true even before the fall of oil prices took effect, because most airlines use the practice of hedging. Most airlines had already agreed to purchase fuel at a set price, so even with the fall of oil prices, that drop did not have a positive effect on the airlines' bottom line until later.

Many monopolies are allowed to persist, because supporting competition in certain industries would be more problematic than helpful. Utility companies are the greatest example of this. While some may be willing to accept this as simply one isolated aspect that needs to be propped up, I see it as yet another affirming example of how capitalism does not work and is not in our best interest. So instead of having the supposed benefit of competition, for one of the most crucial services that we depend upon no less, we are resigned to accept a monopoly. In AISE there would also be a monopoly for this service, but the key difference is that in capitalism the driving force is for the utility company to exploit consumers for as much as they can in order to maximize profits. In Altruistically Inspired Societal Economics there is no concern for such exploitation, as the utility company merely exists to provide the best service possible to the populace. There is no self-serving ulterior motive of profit. The common defense of capitalism is that it is equitable, in that people will pay what they feel the good/service is worth and will not pay any more. Yet that's not exactly true. It is quite frequent where people pay more than they believe the good to be worth, because it is either absolutely necessary or there is no reasonable alternative. As the good becomes higher in necessity or a total lack of any viable substitute exists, then the cost of the good/service usually reaches greater levels of profitability. When is the last time you looked at your utility bill and thought "Wow, what a great value!"

In May 2015 Charter acquired Time Warner Cable. AIG was "too big to be allowed to fail". GE controls everything from media to financing to energy production. How are such conditions good for the consumer? Yet capitalism does not offer any protection from these events. It requires regulation and oversight, two tools that are despised by free market advocates everywhere, to prevent such circumstances. Some complain about how regulation is stagnating the economy or capitalism. What are regulations stagnating, other than the one percent's ability to exploit us? It is amazing that some people decry regulation, but become incensed when it is discovered that companies have been knowingly pumping toxic waste into a neighborhood or ignoring the use of carcinogenic materials in baby items because to do so was more cost effective and therefore more profitable. The reason regulations exist is because these corporations have proven they will ignore the negative impact of their actions, unless they are specifically ordered not to.

If this book is to be criticized for being idealistic, it is beyond idealistic to believe that the majority of profit-driven companies will conduct themselves in an ethical and responsible manner when given total freedom from regulation and enforcement. It is just downright idiocy to believe, despite the dearth of evidence to prove otherwise, that companies will make the ethical (less profitable) choices on a consistent basis. Businesses are not going to do things that are less profitable unless they have to. If a decision is expected to cost them a great deal of money because of a lawsuit or boycott, then of course they will choose a different path, but this again is based on profitability, not ethical value.

Do we really believe that individual industries do not withhold or even subvert public opinion to forward their interests? Do we really accept every tidbit of data fed to us by a particular industry about how fantastic its product is for us? Didn't the tobacco companies insist for years that they had conducted impartial research and determined that there were no worthy health concerns or issues about addictiveness? If you do a Google search for a particular product or service you will typically find as many negative facts or opinions as you do positive ones. Companies have been known to create or pay others to fake consumer experiences to influence consumer ratings. There is currently a great deal of speculation and debate regarding how much the NFL did or did not know regarding the effects of concussions. I am not insinuating anything, but would anyone be shocked if they had tried to protect their multi-billion dollar business model by being less than forthcoming with the medical research?

Further it is hard to argue how proprietary information does not stagnate development. Particularly in industries like medical research. How many different companies and research organizations are protecting their intellectual rights to successful, but incomplete discoveries? How sad would it be if the cure for cancer was in our hands, if not for the fact that the key breakthroughs were being tightly and secretly held by separate groups? Is it really irrational to believe that if all the medical research was pooled together and shared openly, that we would be much closer to a cure or at least prolonging lives? Do we really believe that every scrap of medical research data is just sitting on the internet for one to Google search and add together with all of the other existing data? Is it hard to believe that profit driven corporations are at this moment holding proprietary information that no other groups of researchers are privy to? Imagine the advancements in technology and improvements to human care that total collusion would create, instead of the fragmented and exploitive system we have now. Of course major businesses are more than happy to collude when it results in greater profit, as we have already talked about.

Capitalism can actually impede progress when it threatens the financial success of an individual entity or an entire industry. Whether one believes that there is any overt resistance or not, doesn't it just make sense that big oil companies would not be enthralled with the sudden development of a cheaper and cleaner fuel source? For every great advancement that replaces an older technology, technique, or product there is a group of people that stand to lose their current and future standing. This creates resistance to the change, not based on what is best for society or the environment, but based purely on the desire to continue producing current levels of profitability. In such instances the profitability of the new advancement must have a high enough expectation, to garner enough support to fight off the resistance of the status quo. While it is popular to celebrate how capitalism helps to fuel advancement, capitalism can just as effectively hinder it.

While monetary compensation is not the sole motivator for choosing a profession it has certainly negatively affected this decision making process. Consider that most high paying jobs include a selfish aspect to them. In contrast, jobs that require a high degree of selflessness or willingness to sacrifice for the benefit of society pay poorly. Why is this? It's because we know these people are motivated by a higher purpose and so they will take on said profession despite the low pay. The profession itself calls for self-sacrifice and so we exploit that by making these people sacrifice the possibility of making a better wage. The social worker is given a ridiculous workload for minimal pay, because we know he/she is motivated by higher ideals to begin with. Essentially these are the very altruistic qualities that will make AISE successful. Capitalism abuses those with these qualities, thereby effectively discouraging others. Then supporters of capitalism point to the absence of those with the requisite altruistic qualities to make AISE work.

Other professions are motivated more by greed and personal gain. These professions would not be undertaken if not for the higher wages. Why would one work long hours and be a social pariah for getting rapists set free on technicalities, if not for a high salary? One might argue with the medical doctor, but as honorable as it is to want to save another person's life, there are other factors that make the profession less than enviable. There is a lot of time for schooling and training, it is high stress, and has very long work hours. This makes the high salary necessary. So then does one become a doctor because of the promise of financial reward or the positive social implications?

I am not foolish enough to believe that every poor person has a heart of gold and that every person with more than X amount of dollars in their bank account is morally devoid. As if there were some magical dollar amount at which this transition happened. That is not my point and the point is not to create animosity and division, but to eliminate such boundaries. I don't think that lavishing the lazy is any better than giving a sports contract to a wife-beater. I don't believe in giving free hand outs to everyone either. I'll delve into this more later, but for now please understand that my point is that capitalism only rewards for exceptional physical contributions. Mundane contributions, while every bit as necessary, are only marginally compensated and commonly treated with disdain. A person's worth as a human being is ignored in capitalism.

I'm generalizing here, in that in the purest form, we are equals and we should be treated as such. Certainly the person who refuses to work or the malingerer has no place in AISE any more than in capitalism. Nor is the pedophile to be released from prison and given all the same financial benefits as his victims. I'm describing the rational state in between the two extremes. Neither the dehumanizing capitalist order based solely upon monetary potential nor the naïvely damaging extreme liberal beliefs that people do not need to be held accountable for their actions, no matter how reprehensible or damaging. I'm referring to the law abiding citizen who works diligently, being treated just as well as other law abiding citizens who work diligently. One of these people should not be given obscene levels of compensation compared to others, who through their own actions, are no less worthy of the same compensation. They should all be equally compensated.

Another way in which we have been desensitized to the dehumanization of capitalism is the practice of risk assessment. Risk assessment is nothing more than a mathematical calculation of the probability that an incident will occur. The likelihood that the incident will occur and the most likely dollar value of the punitive action are calculated. The value of human suffering and loss of life is reduced to a formula. It should be a matter of soulfully desiring to preserve life and avoid human suffering. Tough choices would still need to be made in AISE, as no human endeavor can realistically endure indefinitely without some mistake occurring. Yet a decision made with human life being the focal point, rather than monetary value being that focal point is preferable. Currently though, it is transformed into a sterile calculation based on the imaginary constructs of fiscal policy. No longer is the vision of a mangled person the deterrence. Instead the determining factors are the economic loss which such a vision would likely generate through lawsuits, post incident product modification costs, and having to task marketing resources to stave off public backlash.

Mistakes happen. We are human. This will be the case regardless of the economic system we choose to incorporate. The difference is that in capitalism, more often than not, fear of the financial losses due to a mistake outweigh the fear of causing human suffering. As long as accumulated losses as a result of the mistake are deemed likely to be less than the cost of a recall, then so be it. There is the rare and noble instance like Johnson and Johnson's handling of the 1982 tampering with Extra-Strength Tylenol. Even though I was a naïve child not concerned with such adult matters at that time, I still remember what a monumental decision that was; a major corporation that actually chose to place consumer concerns above the drive to make a profit.

Now some will point to this and say, "There you go. A shining example of the good that capitalism can produce." Sadly there is a lot wrong with that sentiment. The decision was made in spite of capitalist teachings, not as a positive side effect of them. James Burke, who was the company's chairman at the time of the incident, deserves praise for making the morally correct choice, but that decision could not have been easy. With the prognosticating by most economic experts that the loss of public trust and the financial cost of the recall would doom the company, there must have been tremendous pressure to seek a safer fiscal option. The company stock value bounced back very quickly and the proper handling of the incident actually increased public perception and support for the company. But during those first few months, when stock values and revenue plummeted, there must have been a great deal of doubt and fear as to whether or not the right choice had been made.

The problem is that we celebrate such a choice, because the very economic system we choose to support, mounted huge influence for him to make a different choice. We do not offer effusive praise for a doctor who makes the moral choice not to molest his patients. Of course not, he is expected not to and it is illegal for him to do so. Johnson and Johnson had done nothing wrong, if anything they were the victims of a criminal act. The point here is that not only were they under no obligation to recall the product and suffer the economic loss that they did, but according to capitalism they really shouldn't have. This is an example of a company doing the right thing, but more often than not companies allow the capitalist influences to convince them not to. We should implement an economic system that would not present moral challenges like capitalism does. In AISE the sole motivating factor would be making the choice that would ensure public safety. There would be no profit margin or stock value consideration to tempt one to pick the immoral or less humanitarian choice.

Most employers during the time that capitalism has been practiced, have seen laborers as nothing more than an asset at best, a hindrance toward profitability at worst. We have only to look at the staggeringly callous and widespread use of sweatshops by profit driven companies throughout the course of capitalism, to include at this very point in time to know this is true. Companies continuously look for loopholes to employ the lowest cost laborers as possible. Of course the justification is always that they need to manage costs in order to be able to provide a quality good for a reasonable price. No mention is made of the funding of exorbitant executive salaries and benefits. Do they really all need to fly first class and stay in five star hotels for a semi-annual "business convention"? Let's not be naïve in thinking that most of these major corporations are just trying to eke out a subsistence. As if the difference of being in the black or the red is a matter of a few hundred dollars. BP, Chevron, ConocoPhillips, Exxon Mobil, and Shell reported *profits* of $93 billion in 2013. Many of these large corporations are looking to expand profit *margins*, not just make a profit. It's the difference between you trying to save $1,000 this year or an *additional* $1,000 this year.

We accept this explanation of cost control because we realize that with our finite and typically already spread out budgets that we cannot afford a $50 box of cereal or a $200 bath towel. So we support the practice and mindset so that we don't have to pay prices like that. Which is good…unless you happen to work in the cereal or bath towel industries. Of course eventually the same mindset and practice hits our own particular industry. Whether it is agriculture, entertainment, or technology; cost cutting by way of decreasing wages, workforce, or benefits is inevitable. Sadly it is only at that moment that we're willing to acknowledge how destructive and damaging it is. Some would acknowledge that this is in fact a problem, but say there is no way to fix it. They would insist that it simply is an integral problem within capitalism and there is no avoiding it. I would agree. That is exactly my point. This is a major problem that causes undue and unnecessary hardship for most of the population not once or twice, but multiple times over the course of a person's lifetime. This causes stress in relationships, creates depression, fosters fear, forces people to forego medical treatments because of loss of benefits, and many other negative side effects. Why do we inexplicably continue to support a system that has such major failings built into its very fabric? Why not seek out a more stable system that eliminates the employer/laborer relationship altogether?

In AISE profit does not drive production decisions. Since goods and services are equitably dispersed, there is no unnecessary driving up of costs so that the one percent can live luxuriously. The equitable distribution also means that consumers do not need to limit consumption based on goods being too expensive. As long as it is agreed, as a society, that certain working conditions are possible and acceptable then the working conditions for each industry are established. There is no threat of diminishing these working conditions for the sake of profit or a lack of funding. Further, this means there is no fear of diminished wages or benefits as everyone will equitably share in the produced goods and services. The workforce can simply be redistributed to accommodate increased or decreased levels of demand for particular goods or services. So barring a societal emergency there should be no need to have unemployment or overworking of the labor force. Isn't this the very problem we run into constantly in capitalism? Capitalism fails us, the 99%, in so many ways. Practically every business or economic choice in capitalism is hinged on whether the one percent should make a profit or be morally responsible to society. Not surprisingly they often pick the former instead of the latter. We have been told so many times that capitalism is so beneficial to us. Unless that "us" is the one percent, I do not see how capitalism is beneficial.

A common theme here is the failing of the highly touted supply and demand paradigm. Another example of this is that it actually does not run as efficiently as the one percent would have you believe. As soon as it is determined that there is a product or service that has significant promise of great profit, everyone clamors to exploit it. The pioneers of this new product have likely had more hurdles to leap and complications to overcome in the developmental stages and the normal process of working out the bugs. The last ones to enter the market risk not even having their business running before the demand (and price) fall off. So there is a limited window of opportunity which is affected by many factors. Eventually the increase of suppliers will exceed the amount of demand and thus force business operators to lower costs, meaning decreased profitability, meaning they have to lay off workers. Typically the winners are the large corporations that copy the business model created by the pioneers. Even in the rare example where they need to buy the rights from the developer of the product, it is still profitable in the long term and only the originator will probably profit. The sheer size of the major corporations allows the lower profit margins to still be a worthwhile venture, since cumulatively it is a significant amount of money. The increased risk of regional limitations and less overall profit amounts make it more difficult for the small business. All of this serves to create turmoil in the workforce and many failed businesses. In the end, the one percent profits, again, and we see the continued proliferation of mega-corporations that pay the least amount of wages. This is one reason why we constantly see businesses failing. How is the social upheaval, personal stress and loss, and wasteful use of resources good for society? With AISE resources could be properly allocated to meet increasing demand for the new product or service. If demand were to be diminished later, for whatever reason, those workers and resources could simply be efficiently repurposed.

Whereas most industrialized nations define poverty as a set percentage difference in amount of income from the median level (relative poverty), in America it is defined as the minimal amount needed to provide for adequate subsistence (absolute/extreme poverty). This means that if the average person in Spain makes $30,000 a year, the poverty level would be anything less than $15,000 a year. In the U.S. we don't care what the average person makes. We just figure what it costs to pay for the absolute basic necessities of life and set that as the poverty level, which is currently $12,000. So while most other countries believe that poverty should be measured in a manner that takes into consideration the ability of the average person at that time to accumulate wealth, Americans are content to simply acknowledge the ability to provide the minimum amenities, despite the level of comfort experienced by the rest of society. This should come as no surprise since capitalism is designed to protect the wealth of the one percent. Why would they want to estimate poverty levels in relationship to their own opulence? With this being the case though, the American style should have a lower threshold for defining one as being in poverty and therefore lower rates of poverty. This is because it ignores the rest of society and measures only the individual's ability to meet the minimal subsistence standards.

In this example, in this country $12,000 is the minimum individual income threshold for poverty. Even though the median income for an individual is $26,000 that is irrelevant. As long as someone earns $12,000 or more they should not appear in this statistic. In Germany the relative poverty is considered to be anything less than 50% of $32,000, which is the median income in adjusted U.S. currency. So only those who make less than $16,000 will be considered in poverty. So that in this example, in America there is a range from 0 - $11,999 where one would be classified as being in poverty, but in Germany there is a range of 0 - $15,999 to meet the standard. One would expect a higher poverty rate in Germany since there is a probability that more people will fall into the wider range. Yet sadly the U.S. has a poverty rate more than twice the rate (this takes into account population differences) of Germany, despite the more stringent definition. So if America was to utilize the more considerate distinction of poverty like many of the members of the European Union do, the threshold would rise to $12,999 and we would see an even worse comparison. Historically, America has had higher levels of poverty than the other higher developed countries of the world. Is this really the definition of a "great nation" that you can be proud of?

Now critics may point to the European Union for examples, both good and bad. Greece is likely to be used as an example of why AISE would fail. Yet when you look at Greece's economic structure it is very similar to our own current system. It is pseudo-socialist capitalism. The biggest difference is that they apply a higher level of socialism than we currently do, although the current trend in this country is to do the same thing. The Greek economy is in shambles because they want to hold onto the selfish benefits of capitalism and the dream of vast wealth. They illogically believe that they can simultaneously finance massively expensive social programs. Obviously they are wrong. The financial realities of capitalism and the complexity of how debt works doomed them to failure. It is baffling how we do not recognize that every step we take in the same direction as Greece only guarantees our own eventual failure in the same way. "Free" programs that are as lavish and widely dispersed as they are in Greece cannot be indefinitely sustained while protecting the right of individuals to hoard wealth. What makes AISE feasible is the fostering of a culture of personal desire to altruistically consider the needs of other people. When you alter the cultural mindset of selfishness then these altruistic policies can be successfully realized.

Those who would pick Norway or Finland as examples of how pseudo-socialist capitalism works, would also be mistaken. The poverty level of Finland is 5.5% (relative poverty). That is significantly less than the current rate of 14.5% (absolute poverty) in this country and so they certainly have much to be proud of. Norway has an even better rate of only 1.7%. I agree that they should be congratulated for such a great achievement and much of this stems from the very cultural mindset that is required in AISE. In both of these countries and others that have had similar success they all exhibit a cultural value of altruism rather than selfishness. Yet these numbers have not always been this low. Both of these countries are benefitting from healthy economies at this time. This is not just happenstance and they deserve credit for managing their economies wisely. But as their historical numbers prove and a number of economists agree, a downturn in the economy would have the same kind of disastrous results as we see in Greece. Obviously the degree of the downturn would determine the degree of effect, but the point is that they lack the economic stability that AISE would provide. This is because ASIE is not subject to the destructive effects of wealth generation (inflation, interest rates, profit margins, cost thresholds) that are an integral part of capitalism. I applaud them for their effort, but this success is precarious and it is the capitalist aspect of their economies that makes it precarious. Lastly, all their success means very little to the 5.5% or 1.7%, respectively, of their populations. Would living in poverty in a moderately pseudo-socialist capitalist country make any difference to you versus living in poverty in a highly pseudo-socialist capitalist country? AISE only tolerates 0% poverty rates, which I'm sure the 14.5% of Americans, 5.5% of Finns, and 1.7% of Norwegians would all equally prefer.

The Myth of the Food Shortage

*If I were to remain silent, I'd be
guilty of complicity.*

Albert Einstein

As of 2014 there were 48.1 million people living in food insecure households in the U.S. There are over 60,000 food banks, pantries, programs, and charities to combat hunger in this country. Think about this for a second. Is this really an epidemic or some easily transmittable disease? When is the last time your local grocery store ran out of food? Doesn't our government actually pay farmers to *not* farm? We can make all the nonsensical excuses we want, but the stark naked truth is that we choose to allow starvation to persist in our country in order to support the continuation of capitalism. There is no shortage of food. In fact there is plenty of food to feed everyone in this country right now. There is no reasonable explanation why there is even one starving person in this country, much less 15.3 million hungry children, as there currently are.

The problem is that we cannot just feed everyone, because to do so would destroy the very capitalist economic system that we cling to. We say that it would cost too much to feed everyone in the country. In purely monetary terms that is true, because of how the fiscal system operates. As you spend more money to feed everyone, you then have less of it to spend elsewhere. You can print more money so you would have more to use, but that only serves to devalue all the currency. Forcibly manipulating lower prices on everything, to allow the money to be spread out more is not only totally contradictory to free market ideals but it also would devalue the currency. In either case the solution then would be to print more money, which would only exacerbate the negative by-product of devaluation.

I understand, and agree, that we cannot simply provide free food or even just allow farmers to overproduce, again because of the problems created by this wondrous free market system. If we were to simply produce and then dump our excess food onto third world nations in need, it would obliterate any impetus for the development of an indigenous agriculture or livestock industry. This is because they would then be effectively competing against a zero cost competitor. Who would want to purchase food from a local farmer if they could get free shipments of grain from the U.S.? Even if they needed to supplement from the local supplier it would likely be in considerably smaller amounts and thereby limit the level of expansion possible by the individual farmer and the local industry as a whole. Likewise, by flooding the domestic market with free food to feed the hungry, it would lead to a sharp loss in profitability, as there would be less incentive to pay for food when one could get it for free. Food prices would also plummet and cause farmers and anyone involved in the production or sale of food to go broke. In our current society and economic system it is inevitable that people would seek out ways to take advantage of the existence of free food being distributed. In fact it is currently a problem with the various programs designed to provide food for those who qualify.

Now some will mistakenly compare this demonstration of exploitation as a sign of why Altruistically Inspired Societal Economics cannot work. The problem is the lack of acknowledgement that it requires society as a whole to change its values and mindset to the promise of equitably sharing, but as compensation for each individual's effort. This is opposed to our current system which preaches that each member is on his/her own. Thus it fosters the very traits which we loathe; greed, exploitation, and desire to get greater value for our effort. If you do not gain for yourself, no one else will. So whether it is by looking for a sale, getting something for free, or stealing; capitalism encourages this behavior. So we foster that fear and need for everyone to fend and gather as much as possible for themselves. We glorify those who amass great wealth and shame those who do not. We say we do not like these negative virtues, but then through our actions and the support of capitalism, we nurture these same qualities. It is much like the mother who hates the screaming tantrums of her child, but then rewards the child with candy to placate him. She wants the behavior to stop, but instead nurtures it with her actions.

In the monetary terms of capitalism it is impossible to end starvation. We cannot "afford" to address these humanitarian concerns in our own country. Yet we are amused and entertained at how 30 seconds of *advertising* during the Super Bowl costs over $1 million. Let us not even get into a debate over welfare right here, talk about abuses of the system, or malingering. I'm talking about wounded and traumatized veterans, people with debilitating disabilities, kids with terminal illnesses that we can't "afford" to take care of properly because we don't have enough funding. But this very same system that we support totally allows for spending millions of dollars...to advertise. I understand this makes sense within the confines of capitalism. The beliefs and rituals of a religion make sense within the confines of the belief system, but looking at these beliefs and rituals as an outsider they may seem mystical or ridiculous. I ask you to think about spending money on advertising not through the lens of capitalism. It makes no sense to use limited funds intended to help people in need, on advertising. But this is capitalism and we accept it. Please ask yourself how this is satisfactory on a humanitarian level. Don't justify it because that is how the system works. Try to justify it purely on its humanitarian value.

While ending starvation is inconceivable within the constraints of capitalism, it does not mean that the act itself is still impossible. When one removes the monetary cost from the equation, what is left? Time and labor. Money is not gasoline. It is not as if the tractor won't work unless we pour money into the tank. The factories, power plants, and water systems all work regardless of whether money is being spent or not. This is difficult to grasp since we've all been brainwashed into believing that money makes the world go around.

> *Labor, it must always be remembered, and not any particular commodity, or set of commodities is the real measure of the value both of silver and of all other commodities.*

Adam Smith

This is a quote from Adam Smith, in reference to poor historical record keeping, causing historians to over or under value commodities in the past, in reference to the valuation of his time. This is about the only thing that Smith says that I can agree with and it is the very basis of AISE. He unwittingly acknowledges that it is actually true that the "costs" we attribute to various services and goods are totally arbitrary. That in fact it can, and in my estimation should, be based purely upon the value that we place on labor. He is acknowledging that that it is irrelevant whether we paid someone $.50/hour to dig a hole 10 years ago and now pay them $40/hour to dig a hole. The only true worth is in what we value that labor to be in how it fits into our current need or desire to be done. So, to Smith, it is less important what the hole digger is paid in monetary sums, than how important we value the labor of digging holes to be in relationship to other current labor needs. In his frustration with the poor record keeping, he acknowledges that the levels of prices and wages established by the one percent of varying points in history are in fact arbitrary. He clearly states that labor is the only true measure of valuation.

Taking this thought process to the next level, we can remove the price tags we have placed upon ourselves to signify our worth. After all isn't that exactly what we do when we say she deserves $28/hour and he deserves $32/hour? We need to stop using a person's ability to generate money as our method of assessing a person's value and acknowledge the worth of each of as human beings. Then we can redefine the value of that labor in a totally new, more humane way. Food and necessary services are not "too expensive". They are only too expensive because we accept the current system of valuation that makes it so. As soon as we convince ourselves of the necessity and ability to move onto to a superior methodology of economics then these false assumptions cease to exist.

So the farmer's time and labor are not too costly, because his time and labor are recompensed by providing him with an equitable portion of the services and goods produced by the whole of the society. There is no inflation or devaluation to be concerned with. How have we gotten to a point where we defend an economic system and way of life that entices and motivates people to stop producing food, in a world where people are starving? How have we gotten to the point that our souls and our minds are in such a state of discord with each other? There are literally thousands of charitable organizations that get funding to fight hunger, many focused on citizens of this very country, and yet the solution is to simply acknowledge the moral shortcomings of our current economic system.

Adam Smith acknowledges this very conundrum. Once again his only concern is how the one percent will gain from this issue rather than being concerned by the negative societal impact. Doesn't it concern you, how the author of the blueprint for our current economic system consistently defends the failings of his own system for the benefit of the one percent? He talks about how the Dutch make a practice of burning spices in order to ensure there is not an "overabundance" which would cause the prices to fall below their *desired* level. He doesn't even say profitable, but *desired*. Smith supports the wasting of resources so that the one percent can squeeze the *desired* amount of profit from the consumer. He also cites the Virginia and Maryland tobacco farmers using the same practice. It is yet another example of how the regurgitated supply and demand relationship is far from being as simple as we have been made to believe. So people are starving in the world and this very country, not due to some famine, but because WE CHOOSE to embrace an economic system designed to manipulate the supply of vital goods and services so that the one percent can achieve higher levels of profit.

Take the food shortage issue to the next level. Currently we, simultaneously bemoan the presence of starving people in the world and the overabundance of cheaply produced unhealthy food. The current status of agriculture and ranching was brought about to overcome food shortage which is one of the greatest hurdles that humankind has had to contend with historically. Floods, droughts, frosts, etc. have destroyed untold amounts of crops and thereby also caused the death of many people. There has been an understandable desire to increase the productivity of agriculture throughout history. Each successful agricultural innovation has been lauded for the security and prosperity that it subsequently bestowed upon humankind. Irrigation, fertilization, and farming tools are arguably the most important developments in human history. Sadly the latest innovations have hinged more upon unnatural manipulations and again that deplorable and soul-killing motivator...profit. It is not that natural methods no longer work, it is that they are not as profitable as the easy chemical and hormone solutions. We accept that corporations have determined that our health and tampering with nature are less important considerations than their ability to produce more profit. It is not that there is a shortage of capable or willing workers. People everywhere are doing their own farming again and the unemployment rates refute the assertion of a lack of available labor.

One only needs to look at the proliferation of communal farms, small local farms, and even the individual household "farming", to see the desire for more natural farming methods. This is all celebrated as the people taking the supply factor into their own hands and taking charge of the system. This is a farce. Historically the large farms were born from their more efficient ability to produce greater amounts of food. This also had the desired ancillary effect of allowing more people to now specialize in and focus on other areas of study. It used to be necessary for the largest portion of society to be farmers, to guarantee that there would be enough to feed everyone. Even so, that usually was no guarantee. With greater technological advancements and techniques we could now feed the whole population with just a fraction of the population serving as farmers.

What served as the pinnacle of human evolution is now being eroded. Humans could finally focus, as a whole, on greater endeavors and innovations in a myriad of fields rather than spending the majority of their lives focused on generating enough food. We are essentially devolving as an increasing portion of the population reverts to attempting to inefficiently, and often ineffectively, farm for themselves. The typical home garden does not produce enough food to eliminate the need for that family to go to the grocery store for its produce, much less all of its food. It is supplemental at best, a waste of time and resources at worst, but more often than not it is just a nice sentimental gesture that is in actuality less efficient than having just bought the groceries. It is also an elitist endeavor as commonly the people who are doing this happen to have enough property and/or the time and resources to dedicate to such activity. But don't mistake lack of action with a lack of desire, it's simply that those who do it happen to have both desire and the current fiscal capacity to do so. In an AISE society, the desire for a return to natural farming techniques is no problem as the necessary workforce size can be easily determined. Since there is such a widespread desire for natural farming, finding those who want to pursue that endeavor would be easy. The difference is that these ineffective individual efforts can once again be efficiently and synergistically combined, so that we are not wasting resources and time.

There is clearly a strong and widespread desire for more natural and responsible food production, yet the majority of the food in this country continues to be highly processed and there is almost a war on the propagation of natural seed production. Heirloom seeds will eventually be a myth if things are allowed to progress the way they are. This conversation could fill its own book. For the purpose of this discussion though it is enough to recognize that large companies want to control the future evolution of being able to grow food. The reason of course is because it is highly profitable. Whereas previously if you took care of a plant/tree and saved the seeds, you could conceivably never need to buy those seeds or that food again. Now that heirloom seeds are almost nonexistent, the companies that produce these seeds guarantee that people will have to come back to them continuously to buy new seeds. This *is* capitalism. These companies manipulate technology and circumstances to produce further profit. They now *own* the ability to create food by controlling seed production and distribution.

Why isn't, Smith's simplistic and often regurgitated mantra of supply and demand not coming to fruition? Because the system itself is flawed. Smith's assertions of supply and demand are in fact too simplistic and do not account for the complexity of the free market concept. Why are we still driving around in gas guzzling cars and using energy production methods that rely heavily upon fossil fuels despite the massive public appeal for alternative fuel sources? Why aren't medical costs and distribution of those services meeting the demand? How about something as simplistic as cable T.V. which has been derided for decades with regard to the almost contemptuous treatment of its consumers? There has been a demand for cable service to improve, yet it has not.

What the infantile explanation that we have all been spoon-fed for so long, fails to acknowledge is that the suppliers do in fact have a considerable amount of influence on the supply and demand relationship. It's amazing how empowered one feels when one hears the supply and demand paradigm. Wow, lowly me has the power to control the direction of industry. I have the power to dictate the path of production choices by simply choosing the good or service of my preference. Pretty heady stuff. The truth is that it only applies to products and services that either have high discretionary value or where there are a number of competitors that offer goods with a common price and quality value.

Do you have trouble accepting that the controllers of resources and production can shift the supply and demand relationship to their favor? How else do you explain the insanity of people murdering and enslaving each other over diamonds when there is no actual shortage of the substance? Most people are now well aware of this fact, yet despite this totally illogical thought process, diamond prices remain exceedingly high. People continue to pay those prices and they continue to accept that this all fuels deplorable human behavior in the quest to reap the contrived monetary benefits that people apply to diamonds. If Smith and the capitalist supporters are correct, then why aren't diamond mines popping up and the supply of diamonds being increased to meet the demand? I thought the supply and demand relation was supposed to be self-correcting and equitable. Apparently not.

In any industry there will be a cost to change the established methods of production. These methods usually came into being in order to increase efficiency, in other words profitability. Most corporations are going to be reluctant to take on the cost of retooling and risking a drop in efficiency. Therefore they employ lobbyists to gain support in slowing or blocking policies that would make change necessary. By slowly creating change, they can then charge exorbitant prices for the desired goods. The high prices acts as a deterrent to those who want the good, particularly when a less expensive alternative still exists. We see this with food. More naturally grown food has a demand, but the availability of cheaper less healthy food provides an alternative that many will settle for out of necessity. Again we see how producers control price and demand by controlling supply. As long as there are enough people willing, and more importantly, able to pay the higher prices for what is actually demanded then it is profitable for the corporation to continue producing these goods in limited fashion. So you can have the healthy food, but it is going to cost significantly more. It is more profitable and less risky to sell the lower quality food though. By keeping the bulk of the business caught in this low risk, easy profit segment, corporations are willing to tolerate the smaller portion of higher risk and more costly business of organic food.

As we have already explored, this is where capitalism actually hinders advancement, or in this case it's actually a retro movement. Those in control of resources do have the ability to manipulate supply and therefore price, despite the demand of society. Smith acknowledges as much and even supports it. All this is because the large corporations that stand to lose a lot of money are manipulating policies and supplies in an effort to prevent the change of direction that society wants. We fear socialism because a handful of people will supposedly make all the decisions regardless of the will of the people. We've already established how this thinking is misplaced, but regardless, how is allowing a handful of CEOs the same exact power any better? The idea of an oligarchy abusing socialism to control us is detestable, so we choose to embrace democracy that is corrupted by capitalism thus making a de facto oligarchy. So we unwittingly support the very problem that we say we are avoiding.

Why Capitalism Guarantees Democracy Will Fail

*Let us not seek the Republican
answer or the Democratic
answer. Let us not seek to fix
the blame for the past. Let us
accept our own responsibility
for the future.*

John F. Kennedy

Few, if any, of us do not recognize or voice our displeasure at the flaws of our government. Yet we fail to recognize how capitalism and the greed for personal gain that it fosters is responsible for most of these flaws. Instead, we turn to charitable acts, volunteer groups, and nonprofit organizations to laud our worth as a people. As if these altruistic concepts somehow demonstrate the greatness that capitalism can bring out. The irony is that what we point to as proof of our caring humanitarian side, is the exact opposite of capitalism. We hail our charity organizations like beacons of light to demonstrate our moral greatness. As if to say, "Look, despite our overwhelming need to be greedy and selfish we *choose* to give stuff away for free!" We enthusiastically defend a system that creates people who are "have nots" and then we pat ourselves on the back for being caring enough to give them pocket change. If charity and sacrificing to make these people's lives better really is something that we are proud of and think is respectable, then why do we practice a system that is designed to completely ignore a person's human value in the first place? Let's race up this mountain. If I see you start to fall, I'm not going to do anything about it though. But because I'm a great guy, after I make it to the top, I'll throw down my first aid kit to you. If I actually was a great guy, wouldn't I prevent you from suffering in the first place? Instead of letting you fall and break 16 bones so that I could "win" first? Then, when I do show how caring I am, it's not like I'm going to do anything that really solves your problems.

How is it good that most people are spending 40-60 hours a week trying to acquire as much wealth as possible and then just a few hours volunteering or donating a small amount each week? Isn't this backwards? Shouldn't we be spending the majority of our effort making sure these veterans, senior citizens, and special needs kids are cared for and only a minority of effort trying to accumulate wealth? We're grasping at straws so that we don't have to see the reality that what we are actually doing is counterintuitive to what we profess to believe. We Facebook about how incensed we are that a certain group is not being properly cared for, is being exploited, or needs more support. Then we defend capitalism and go off to work so we can accumulate more personal goods and wealth. I get it. If we don't individually make money to support ourselves, then we will be the ones in need. But we make it easy on ourselves too. By supporting capitalism we can then just point and blame others for these problems. It's the fault of the lazy people, the government, or a lack of sufficient funding. That's life, what do you do? You look for a viable solution that rectifies these humanitarian wrongs that most of us clearly acknowledge.

Our solutions are about as effective as putting a band-aid on a gunshot wound, because even with these charitable causes, there is still a deplorable shortfall in how people are cared for. I'm talking about veterans not being able to get jobs because of disabilities (mental and physical) incurred as a direct result of their service. I'm talking about healthcare not being provided in a timely and effective manner. Our government is ineffective because of the corruptive nature of capitalism and this creates a reliance upon charitable services. While there are wide variations between the most and least efficiently run nonprofits, their overall efficiency is debatable. Not to mention, 89 nonprofits pay their highest executives, salaries between $500,000 and $1 million. Once again, we see how capitalism is more about personal gain than it is for the humane consideration of others. One can point at this too and say here is another example of how even a social program is ineffective. It is only ineffective because it suffers from being forced to exist in an overwhelming capitalist environment.

The Catch-22 is that if a nonprofit is small enough not to be corrupted or overly influenced by capitalism, then it likely does not have a widespread effect. Yet if it becomes large enough to start having the desired altruistic effects, it is then typically corrupted by the capitalist forces seeking to exploit the large amounts of financial resources it then commands. People acknowledge every day how broken our current system is. Welfare abusers, a horrific foster system, the fact that less than one percent of the global population controls an absurd proportion of the total wealth, a healthcare system that miserably fails to provide for everyone, starving people, political corruption, corporate malfeasance, lobbyists who buy votes and influence legislation through financial coercion, major corporations acting with impunity- do I need to continue? This is the system that we're vehemently defending? Upholding a system this rife with deplorable acts of human behavior is really better than giving serious and due consideration to a more humane and effective system?

We allow our wounded veterans to suffer and receive inadequate care. The most recent, and ongoing, scandal involving the Department of Veterans Affairs is a direct result of a lack of adequate funding. The ensuing cover up was a result of that and an attempt to maintain political favor. This allowed the administration to ignore the hard choice of having to request more money to provide adequate services and risk losing funding for some other program they deemed more important.

In all fairness, every administration has to make these kinds of choices due to monetary constraints created by capitalism, but as a veteran this particular example is especially upsetting. If this had all been made clear from the outset there would have been more clamor to allot more funds, which would have then required a higher budget. This in turn would have forced the administration to either ask for a lot more money or to trim the budget in other areas. Now I'm certainly not excusing this reprehensible behavior and firmly believe that all involved deserve to be incarcerated as criminals, no matter their political rank. I am merely pointing out that if not for the shortages that capitalism creates, this choice would be more easily handled in the first place.

We know, and accept, that government funded programs are not sufficient on their own to properly address the issues at hand. When you consider that though, it makes no sense. The very purpose of handing over authority and responsibility of a specific concern to the federal government is to eliminate the need for profit generation and to bring the full weight of the nation to bear against the issue. After all, the federal government is supposed to represent the combined will and financial influence of the nation, rather than an individual, company, or state. Some will say this is the prime example of why AISE wouldn't work. This is incorrect.

The problem is that the whole system has been corrupted with the lure of power and financial gain. Lobbyists making promises and "donations" in return for programs, policies, or contracts that favor the interests of the people the lobbyists represent. Everybody uses lobbyists today. Even local jurisdictions have begun to employ firms, with tax payer money, to go to Washington to make sure that their interests are given consideration. So we have local elected officials using our taxpayer money to pay people to go to D.C. to payoff, sorry I mean "lobby", people who were elected to represent my best interests, to represent my best interests. Really? Yes, this is true. The result is a hyper-inflated budget rife with superfluous costs so that politicians and corporations can increase their wealth and profit margins. Capitalism invites failure in conscientious governing by way of the promise of great personal gain. As that potential increases, as it has over the last few decades in this country, so does the likelihood that those in question will succumb. Having professional politicians only exacerbates this problem. Creating term limits is something that should be implemented, regardless of practicing capitalism or AISE. Even though Altruistically Inspired Societal Economics would greatly reduce this negative influence, when you allow anyone to sit in power for a prolonged period there is a higher risk of corruption.

Corruption is a negative and unavoidable side effect of capitalism. In an economic system that isolates individuals into assuming sole responsibility for their own wellbeing the lure of corruption is extremely high. But when you remove the need to procure wealth in order to care for yourself or to be able to enjoy luxuries the lure of a bribe is significantly decreased. When you are confident that you will be provided for and there is no fear of not being able to pay the mortgage, medical bills, or insurance premiums, there is significantly less leverage to use as enticement. When society has changed its values from that of selfishness and focusing on wealth accumulation to being altruistic and genuinely concerned with the wellbeing of others, it is far less likely that corruption will exist. Who is easier to bribe, the person who believes in what she does and has conviction? Or the one who is worried about how she is going to feed her kids tomorrow? Capitalism all but guarantees the existence of corruption and the greater the amount of available wealth, the greater the probability and degree of that corruption.

The biggest fear of accepting the pseudo-socialist capitalist economy proposed by the Democrats, is that we will simply be ceding further wealth control to the same professional politicians. The same politicians who have proven that they will capitulate to the desires of the special interest factions that use their wealth to get what they want. The Republicans are no different in that respect. *"We the People"* need to stop bickering amongst ourselves. I am guilty of it myself, but we need to stop pointing at the other side and saying "look what they're doing", when "our" side is doing the exact same thing. Whether it is Republicans getting money from the NRA and big oil, or the Democrats getting money from Planned Parenthood and Unions does it make a difference? We're not taking charge and choosing leadership. We're choosing which special interest group we want having more influence. The truth is that it's actually not Democrats versus Republicans. Libertarians or Tea Party members. Liberals versus Conservatives. It's about the one percent getting the other 99% of us to bicker among ourselves to see which side we will let have the greater influence for four years. Until we come to the realization that we ALL benefit greatly from the implementation of Altruistically Inspired Societal Economics and that the only people who will suffer any loss at all is the one percent, nothing is going to change.

Although classical capitalist doctrine says otherwise, capitalism does require that there be guidelines and regulation to prevent abuses, monopolies, and the protection of property ownership, among other things. This must be executed by the government, or some other centrally controlled entity with sufficient influence and authority. This is a fact that even Thomas Jefferson, a staunch anti-federalist, eventually had to concede. A democracy under capitalism relies on the integrity of the members of the governing body to not allow themselves to be swayed into making decisions that would favor select interests, in return for financial gain. This must occur, despite the fact that these members of the government are responsible for their own individual financial survival. Either we pay these people a lot, to insulate them from the influence of lobbyists (as we already do) or we risk having them making decisions in favor of these special interests in exchange for greater wealth (as we already do). So we actually believe that it is realistic that a handful of wealthy people will not allow other wealthy people to influence their decisions by showering them with even greater levels of wealth? Alternatively, AISE is impossible because it is inconceivable that a society could learn to work for the best interests of their fellow man? Here are some undeniable facts about the current situation in this country:

1) Only members or lackeys of the 1% are able to get elected. They are professional politicians, sitting in office for so long that they have no recollection of what it is like to live in the same reality as us.
2) There are wealthy special interest groups that manipulate the politicians to pass policies that serve their interests rather than those of society.
3) Officials are bought right before our very eyes with million dollar "campaign contributions".
4) These politicians make eight times more than the poverty level, so they are completely ignorant to the concerns of the typical American.
5) The ability to determine their own salaries and to guarantee themselves social benefits like retirement and excellent medical coverage, while most Americans do not have any, cause these politicians to look on the plight of typical Americans with indifference.

6) These politicians create conflict among the 99% by taking from some to fund ineffective "social" programs for others. This creates a disgruntled segment pitted against a dependent segment and solves nothing.

This is exactly the situation we are in now. With a democratically elected republic. Under capitalism, allegedly, the greatest economic system ever developed. How is it possible that so much malfeasance and activity contrary to the good of society could possibly manifest itself when we are carefully and responsibly preaching greed, self-preservation, and as much wealth accumulation as possible? I mean these are all noble and responsible pursuits. Why would morally devoid, selfish people be attracted to leadership positions in such an economy? I don't get it. Well here is what a democratically elected republic implementing AISE would look like:

1) There will be no 1% since everyone has equitable amounts of wealth and politicians will have term limits to prevent dynasties and to ensure fresh, real perspectives.
2) There will no longer be wealthy special interest groups. There will be genuine debating and discussion, but not policy that has been bought and paid for.
3) No one will have or be allowed to spend millions on a campaign, so any capable person can realistically run for office without having to sell out to sponsors first.
4) Everyone will be equitably compensated for their labors so disparity would not even exist, your economic concerns are literally everyone's concerns.

5) Everyone will enjoy the exact same social benefits.

6) There will be no 99% to pit against each other.

We should be ashamed at how we have allowed these politicians to become so blatantly corrupt. It will not be much longer before they just come right out and start wearing logos like NASCAR drivers. Political Action Committees and lobbyists are now free to donate unlimited amounts of money to the Democratic and Republican National Committees. How can we know that and not immediately recognize that this is capitalism directly corrupting democracy? If you believe AISE is too idealistic I would propose to you that believing democracy and freedom can actually flourish amidst capitalism is even more idealistic. I have heard repeated assertions that AISE can only function on a limited scale due to the inability of altruistic concern to overcome selfish desires in a broad population. Yet, do you really believe that the elected officials in our broad scale are actually serving the best interests of society? On a limited scale there are examples of those who serve faithfully and are not swayed by corruption. But on the larger scale, no reasonable argument can be made that democracy operates in this country without being influenced by either corruption, corporate interest, or profit seeking motivation.

In AISE everyone is guaranteed equitable distribution of goods and services, including vital necessities and luxuries. While there will still be some personal wealth, the extent of it will be limited, not in the sense of regulated maximum allowable limits, but because when everyone is equitably cared for there is far less need or opportunity to collect and hoard. Massive, privately owned and controlled companies will not exist so there will be less groups applying pressure to secure their interests. There will still be special interest groups, but now they will all stand on equal footing. Law and policy will be influenced by the quality of their legal arguments or by the democratic process of their having larger numbers of supporters than their opposition. Policy will not be determined by who can buy the most politicians, as it is now.

Think about that. A world where politicians cannot buy 90% of the advertising and thereby all but guarantee election because people don't know a thing about the competitor. Whether it is the NRA versus gun control promoters or Planned Parenthood versus pro-lifers, both sides of every argument will get equal voice and due consideration. No more fear of sheer volume of a particular message due to the amount of money brought to bear for a cause. The power of a cause will be returned to the people and not to whomever owns the most media outlets or can buy the most air time. People will make informed decisions when the facts are disseminated evenhandedly. Facts will not be lost amidst the cacophony of massively financed misinformation campaigns. When facts are skewed to favorably present those with greater financial influence, how can we be expected to make informed choices? When AISE eliminates all this, it then comes down to a real democratic decision.

As of 2014, 45 million (14.5%) Americans lived below poverty line. While the average household has a net worth of roughly $66,000 the average senator has a net worth of a little over $1 million. Between the guaranteed excellent healthcare plan, a pension that actually increases, expense accounts, and continued speaking fees, this wealth is all but guaranteed to last the rest of their lives. How long will we continue to foolishly believe the lies that these people tell in order for them to maintain their lavish lifestyles? Every time one of them hears one of us yell how Republicans are worse than Democrats or vice versa, they must collectively giggle. It is amazing how nonpartisan the building becomes when they vote on their own salary increases and benefit plans. I'm not talking about violent revolution, but we need drastic change.

We need to have the courage to demand change. Courage is not exemplified when the path is clear and success is guaranteed. Courage is having the conviction to set a course of action to correct something you know to be wrong. AISE is not perfect, but it is rational, it is possible, and it is right. We fear AISE because a small faction might illegally manipulate the system to gain wealth and exploit the populace. So instead we embrace capitalism in which a small faction *legally* manipulates the system to gain wealth and exploit the populace. Even if one thinks AISE is completely misguided, there is no logical way one can argue that the current system is functioning in a moral and responsible way. If one can demonstrate to me a more ethical and humanitarian system than AISE, I will embrace and espouse it. We should no longer tolerate the demoralizing state that we are in. This is the "land of the free and the home of the brave." Let's act like it.

Conflict Among the Proletariats

*I wonder how many people I've
looked at all my life and never
seen.*

John Steinbeck

There was a widely disseminated story on social media about a classroom economics lesson with regard to test grades and socialism. The professor told the students that he would apply socialism to their grading. After the first test the average was a B so that was what everyone got (Line 1. Graph 1). The students who had studied hard were upset that those who put forth no effort still got a B. The next test, supposedly, everyone failed because no one bothered to study. They had all hoped to enjoy the fruits of other people's efforts (Line 2. Graph 1). This was a misguided and mistaken example. The lesson oversimplified altruistic economic principles in that it provided equality of reward without consideration of effort. The lesson here was that people who are allowed to do nothing at all and still profit will destroy the system. This is true. It is also true that in our current situation we already have people who are really poor AND those who are really rich who do nothing...and will destroy the system. AISE works because all people receive *and* work equitably. This is a critical and yet typically ignored or unrealized facet of AISE. AISE works because the culturally accepted standard shifts the moral value from wealth accumulation and shifts it to altruistic concern. I will discuss this in detail in a later chapter. But this lack of consideration toward the need for everyone to equitably labor, as well as equitably gain, is an infantile representation of AISE in order to foster negativity.

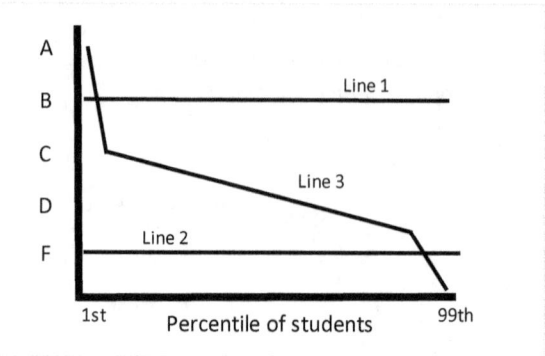

While no one was happy with socialism being a flat horizontal line of equality, no one discussed that capitalism is equally frustrating. The "socialist" line goes straight across because everyone got the same grade, regardless of their effort. In capitalism though only one or two people will get A's, a couple will get B's, some will get F's, but the majority will get C's and D's, regardless of their effort (Line 3. Graph 1). Capitalism guarantees that this will be the outcome as much as this application of socialism guarantees its outcome, but this is totally overlooked. We are led to believe in this example that in capitalism only the "dumb and lazy" will fail. That if you work hard you are then guaranteed an A or financial success. This is not true though, because capitalism cannot function if everyone is a millionaire. There have to be rich people who control capital and those who need capital. Those who need capital are then willing to work for those who control the capital.

Just because one works diligently and perseveres there is no guarantee that one will succeed. So the popular moral to the story is how the students bemoaned everyone getting a B despite there being an inequitable degree of effort by everyone. But capitalism does not guarantee that those who study hard will get their A either. In fact it is more unfair than even the hated bell curve. That is the one where there is only a small percentage that get A's, the majority get decent grades, and a small percentage must fail, all regardless of their effort. Capitalism is similar in that it guarantees that only a small percentage will do extremely well. There may or may not be a portion that do okay, but the majority will need to get C's or D's. There has to be "haves" and "have nots". This is irrelevant to how hard someone works, their dedication, or motivation. Even if everyone gave it 100% effort and the results were all equal in every way, you would, by necessity, still need to have people making significantly less than others.

This is what gets overlooked, because the lie that you *will* be rewarded for your efforts is so widely believed. Are you really telling me that Paris Hilton *earned* her lifestyle more so than the guy who is working three jobs right now? We accept these lies because we need to feel justified in what we do and because of the fear we have of losing what we possess. The mindset becomes: "I must work hard so I do not lose what I have earned. Forget anybody else, I need to protect what I have earned. Someone else may not have received what they earned, but that is not my concern. I earned this and that justifies and reinforces my callousness to the needs of others." In capitalism this callousness to others is what helps us keep our status.

This self-centered divisiveness is what protects the one percent. Look at history and think how many times a small portion of the populace has managed to manipulate and exploit the masses. How is that? By dividing them and creating distrust amongst them. We are encouraged to believe "Other people are lazy, that is why they are poor" and "I work hard that is why I am doing well. I must ignore them and continue to work hard." This is all a lie. It is designed to keep the working segment divided and to support a system that only benefits the one percent. Some of the hardest working, loyal, and dedicated workers I have met, work in jobs that are looked down upon and pay the least. A person's pay does not necessarily reflect their effort. It has become too commonly accepted that poor people are poor because they are lazy. I'm not going to deny that lazy people exist and that they do exploit the system, but they are not the main problem. We have been conditioned so that those in poverty are spiteful toward the middle income segment for their advantage and the middle income segment labels those in poverty as being stupid or lazy. Why are both segments, which make up 99% of the population, not addressing the one segment that could solve all these financial issues instantly? Because the one percent has coerced us into believing these divisive arguments.

Despite the best of fanciful lies that lead us to believe otherwise, capitalism does in fact depend on the establishment of "haves" and "have nots". Capitalism cannot function if we are all considered equals. There has to be a segregation of the population in order to determine who the workers are and who the controllers of production are. There must be a distinction between skilled and unskilled laborers. There must be those who are recognized and treated as superiors to others. In this sense I'm referring purely to their financial worth. This is what capitalism is establishing, tiers of worth based on one's ability to produce fiscal value. There is no consideration given to the fact that we are all human beings deserving of equal respect and recognition. So I am no longer better than you because of racial or hereditary bias, but I am still better than you because I make more money than you. This is progress?

The one percent are dependent upon capital. Capital depends on a wage-labor relationship. This relationship relies on conflict among laborers. Capitalism naturally sets the working segment against itself. The "Walmart Conundrum" is a good example of this dilemma. Admittedly, one of the draws is simply the megastore I-only-need-to make-one-stop benefit. The convenience of it is an excellent idea to be sure. The conundrum lies in the fact that the exact same box of name brand cereal can cost an additional $1 per box at a competing grocery store, than at Walmart. As the bread winner of my family and trying to make the money stretch as far as possible, it is only responsible to buy the cheaper version of the exact same product. This is the very basis of Adam Smith's supply and demand theory. Supporting the economic survival of a rival grocery chain is not going to help guarantee the survival of my family. If I get laid off, the competing grocer is not going to promise to feed my family for having needlessly spent an extra $400 a year on groceries at their store. Due to my own financial restraints the rational choice is to shop at Walmart. This is *exactly* what capitalism says we should all do.

In order to make the best financial choice for my family I need to ignore that this is going to have two very clearly negative side effects. The first, is that the reason Walmart is beating competitors' prices is because they pay their employees less than others do. This is not exactly an industry that is pumping out six figure pension retirees in the first place, so that alone is a powerful consideration. The second, is that as we all follow the capitalist theory, the competitors are being driven out. If the economy worsens, many of those who were choosing to ignore capitalism and shop at the competitors, may be forced to abandon their idealism in the face of necessity. So if the economy were already being bearish, it would likely double the negative impact on these competitors and force them out of business even quicker. Eventually there will be a monopoly as Walmart stands alone. There is certainly precedence to this, as it has occurred repeatedly across the country.

The key here is understanding that this all develops as a result of the proper functioning of capitalism. This is not some random aberration, but it is how capitalism is meant to function. One seller offers identical products at a lower price. According to textbook capitalism, the consumer is supposed to be drawn to this particular seller. Competitors can produce a new product, match the price, or go out of business. Matching the price means cutting wages. This is what capitalism is meant to do. It is meant to pit working segment member against working segment member. I, with my finite funds, seek to find the cheapest product in other industries. But others seek the same lowest cost for goods in my industry. So all of us, in seeking to stretch our money further actually hinder each other. Raising minimum wage has a zero sum effect, because everyone's wages will rise proportionately and so will the prices. The only common facet here is that in all of these scenarios the one percent continue to profit at the expense of the conflict amongst the working segment. The system is ingenious in that people don't typically understand that this is happening. This is because as people look for a better deal they think they're getting over on the industry. "Hah, I got my Frosted Flakes for $.80 off! I just got one over on the cereal makers." No. You likely just contributed to someone's lost overtime or benefits package. Someone like you, who can ill afford such a loss. The cereal makers are going to do just fine. And quite frankly if one cereal maker does go under, there will be another cereal maker or another food industry product maker to take their place. But I guarantee it's not going to be anyone from the working segment that will reap the benefit.

These issues have been further exacerbated as the general populace began to be, in effect, both worker and owner by way of 401ks and other stock options. This has been a great boon for those in power, as it has enabled them to enforce another level of control upon the working segment, while simultaneously exploiting them. The middle income segment has looked upon this opportunity to have some control and the possibility to share in the profits with a very positive attitude. I concede that stock ownership has benefitted some who would not otherwise have been able to amass an equivalent amount of wealth. That being said, it can hardly be demonstrated to have benefitted the majority of the population. If this was true, the widespread participation in 401k and IRA's, combined with the continual record setting highs of the stock market should have resulted in the middle income segment massively widening the gap from the lower income segment. They should also have at least proportionately kept pace with the one percent. Instead, we see the gap between the middle and lower income segments disappearing and the gap widening from the one percent beyond proportional expectations. There are a number of factors that are responsible for this lack of widespread success.

Certainly malfeasance by corporate leaders is a major reason. We have seen over the last two decades criminal activity, albeit from a limited few, but nonetheless it has had staggering and widespread ramifications. These capitalists have brought about financial ruin to countless middle income workers who had been advised to invest in stocks to reap the huge rewards like the big business owners. The truth is that even in these highly publicized crimes the one percent are insulated from the effects and it is the 99 percent of us who are left with the burden of bearing the consequences. But there are also other influences which degrade the ability of the common investment holder from realizing the promised rewards.

Many people find themselves hit by unexpected hardships and are unable to leave a significant portion of their total wealth to sit idly in an investment account. When one is worth billions it becomes far easier to allot funds to investment accounts and in amounts large enough to survive downturns in stock price. The penalties for early withdrawal that are mercilessly and incomprehensibly levied only serve to further damage the already desperate investor. These penalties erode any profit the investor may have made and damage the ability to re-establish the investment. This is a calculated function that allows those in power to continue to squeeze the middle income segment further. There are studies which have revealed that one out of four American households will have to make an early withdrawal from a 401(k) or 403(b) plan and typically these withdrawals are due to necessity. This does not include other retirement vehicles like IRAs or even personally held stocks, which do not have penalties. But the detrimental effect still applies. It is estimated that nearly a third of the money held by the middle income segment for retirement is withdrawn, annually. Between taxes, penalties, and the loss of the compounding interest benefits, the effect is disastrous.

Can anyone logically explain to me the necessity of levying a 50% excess accumulation penalty upon those who fail to withdraw the required minimum distribution from their IRA accounts each and every year after achieving the age of 70 and a half? The government *requires* IRA owners to withdraw specific percentages of their holdings each year after reaching the age of 70 and a half or they penalize them. It is arbitrary penalties such as this that served to only jam salt into open wounds during the stock market crash of 2008. Investors already facing greatly depreciated stock values would have been better served by trying to hold onto these stocks in the hopes that they would recoup value in the future. For those who fell into this unfortunate bracket though, they were actually forced to sell these stocks at a large loss or suffer the penalty instead. Not much in the way of great choices. It is not as if this is the only time this has happened either.

Any investment advisor with a half a brain will advise you not to make plans to make distributions for a given short-term time frame, because of the volatility and unpredictability of the market. For instance, if you want to buy a house in 2020 don't plan on distributing that money in 2020. You should try to distribute the money about 3 years ahead of time and reinvest it in a more stable investment vehicle, like a CD. This way if a market crash, or even just a failing of the particular stocks you are invested in, occurs in 2020, your dreams of a new house don't crash too. Doing this 2 or 3 years earlier gives a person more cushion in case this scenario occurs, because it will likely require at least that much time to recoup losses from such an event. So if a crash happened in 2016 there would be a decent chance that you could recoup your losses by 2020 and still be able to buy the house. So by planning ahead, the dream for the house can stay locked in, despite what market fluctuations occur in the unpredictable future. So if this is a concept that even the most generic financial advisor understands, why is it that the Federal government necessitates common investors to adhere to what is clearly a bad investment practice? They have established rules which require people to take unnecessary risk in a volatile system, so that they are far more likely to incur losses. Do you really think this is a mistake? Do you believe that our Federal government, which is basically controlled by the one percent, doesn't realize the damage that they inflict upon the middle income segment with these ridiculous rules?

The concept of promoting the proletariat class to buy shares of ownership is really quite devious. It sets members of the working segment, unwittingly, against each other. Now as shareholders (read: laser focused profit seekers) the proletariat members now find themselves thinking and acting with the same coldhearted, mathematical, presumption driven quest for the maximum amount of stock growth. They buy and sell stocks, often armed with sparing amounts of fact or data. This is because the data is hoarded by the one percent and also because gathering such data requires massive amounts of time that the typical worker does not have to give. Usually it is also with the singular intent of realizing the greatest amount of stock value over the shortest term possible. The indiscriminant selling of stock holds the same detached sense as those who use credit cards without the appreciation to the underlying monetary reality. The profit-driven buying and selling of stocks affects these individual companies and more poignantly, the workers at these companies. The proletariat now effectively aid the one percent in an effort to relentlessly push workers to the limit in order to maximize their own goal of gaining wealth. The working segment does this by unwittingly following the buy/sell indications spewed out by advisors and self-proclaimed stock experts.

Diversification is a very common investing mantra. If one is too heavily invested in one industry or company and it goes bad, then one can be wiped out. By diversifying one's portfolio, there is a better probability that gains in other sectors will help overcome losses suffered in one particular sector. Yet the common worker who probably does not have or barely has a six figure portfolio to begin with, cannot truly diversify. Spreading one's assets out at such lower levels only serves to dilute possible gains. Telling a worker with limited diversification ability in the first place, not just to invest in the same sector, but the same company that she works for is horrific advice. Now one's income and a growing portion of one's investment power will all be tied to the same company. Not if, but when there is a downturn in that particular company, not only will the worker be facing loss or decrease of benefits and wages, but they will now simultaneously be facing stock value loss at the time they may need it most. Yet employers have been pushing this practice more and more. Why? Let me explain.

The one percent now have free access to the wealth of the proletariat as they invest more and more of their wages (paid by the one percent) into companies owned by other one percenters. In many instances the wages are almost laughably handed right back to the owners through employee stock options. So now they pay money for labor, which is then returned directly back for re-investment. They have created and sold us on a system where they are now getting the same labor for less cost. Even if the stock goes up and you in fact do get rich, it costs the company nothing. This is because when shares exchange hands it is not the company that is paying the stock price, but instead it is whoever chooses to buy the stock from the seller that is paying the cost. In the meantime, if you are getting paid $20/hour and invest 10% in the stock purchase, that means they are really paying you $18/hour and get $2/hour as interest-free investment money from you. So the company now has the capital that it desired and at a significantly reduced cost. This is also not something that really ever gets paid back. Again, it is not the company that pays when the stock is sold. The inflated promise is that the employees now have the opportunity to reap the benefits of their own hard work.

Of course everyone dreamily recounts the story of Microsoft employees who did in fact reap those rewards and use that as irrefutable proof that faith in this system is thereby justified. I know people have survived jumping out of airplanes with defective parachutes, but I would not use these rare examples as justification to start making it a common practice to skydive without a parachute. I would hope that you too would consider this to be an ill-advised justification too. Most financial advisors and those involved in such economic decisions are quick to point out that investing is not gambling. That it is not based on random lucky choices, but educated and informed decisions with the highest probability of a successful outcome. For most common investors though it really is more luck than skill and so pointing to the lucky few does not mean that investing for the common worker actually is a good idea.

By promoting and expanding the involvement of the general public into stock ownership, the one percent has simply gained increased access to an even greater amount of wealth at minimal cost. Think about it. These billionaires, instead of paying interest on a loan, now take your money with no promise and minimal accountability and use it instead. It is clearly established that there is no guarantee of profit to the shareholder and the level of decision making influence is for all intent, nonexistent. Shareholders are by legal definition the last debtors in line. That means every other person who can make a claim of debt against the company at the time of bankruptcy gets paid in full before a single shareholder sees one cent. If that is still vague, let me spell it out. If things go bad, the huge banks and other one percenters are going to get paid first with whatever is left. It is us, the duped proletariats, who will, once again, be the financial losers.

There is a cost in setting up the process of selling shares and getting accepted on a respectable market, but it is negligible compared to the cost of paying interest on a conventional bank loan. Now there is a certain truth to the increased scrutiny and new hoops to hop through when taking a company public. But it is still highly profitable for these companies to sell stock. It is no mistake or happenstance that most publicly traded companies operate in such a way that the shareholders have a negligible effect on how the company is actually managed or the direction that it takes. The idea of ownership or control by common shareholders is, in most instances, preposterous.

This leads to the current state of affairs where the focus is not on actually producing anything, but it is not even about creating a profit in the traditional sense. It is now all about creating derivatives that serve to drive up stock prices, and in many instances it is nothing more than a temporary mathematical illusion. Remember that stock prices do not necessarily reflect the actual fiscal health of a business, but rather the public perception of that company's future value. The most recent economic crisis was a direct result of irresponsible attempts to manipulate numbers to create imagined wealth. Nothing was actually created or built, it was all predicated on clearly precipitous presumptions and an arrogant, and illogical, belief of indefinite sustainability.

Let me elaborate. Company A, for whatever reason, becomes an investment darling. Investment demand increases as people anticipate that in the future this company will do very well. So it behooves them to own the stock now, so that they can maximize their future profit. As demand increases, the price is driven up. This inflated stock price can continue to absurd levels as amateur and/or foolish investors ignore the company's actual capitalization value. These investors start paying prices for the stock that far exceed the company's real net worth. Let's say that the company has money and assets that equal $1 million and sales are expected to have net profits of $200,000 a year. People are paying $100 per share and there are a total of 500,000 shares in circulation.

$100/share x 500,000 shares = $50,000,000 stock value

(stock value) $50,000,000 > $1,000,000   (actual value)

This would mean that the stock value would be 50 times higher than the actual net worth and even expected profits would not close this gap for some time. Demand begins to wane as the luster of promise fades and as the company continues to fail to meet the extraordinary expectations, the price begins to plummet. The company does not even have to be doing badly. In fact the company is making money and is profitable, but because the stock was purchased at such inflated rates it is still a bad investment for the shareholders. Now foolhardy investors sell their deflated shares at a loss and more savvy investors (typically members of the one percent) rush in to buy the shares of a good company at a discount rate. If this seems like a process of convoluted and baseless assumptions being bandied about, without substantive fact to support them, you would be correct. Our economy is essentially based on people's best guess about how well a company will do some time in the future.

Another popular justification for capitalism is the benefit of competition. This is just a different method the one percent employ to create conflict and convince us that it is in our best interest to compete against each other. Such Spartan and adversarial mantras like, "cream rises to the top", "the strong will survive", and "separate the wheat from the chaff" have become part of our lexicon. Those are stimulating analogies, but when you stop and consider that this "chaff" could represent your father with Alzheimer's, would you really dump him on the ground to die like you would just let the proverbial chaff fly away in the wind? These are strong words that are easy to regurgitate until reality strikes. If we, as a society, are truly going to embrace these Spartan ideals, then we should be ashamed of ourselves for our utter moral desolation. Are we going to mercilessly embrace the spirit of these cold-hearted quotes and descend into moral wantonness or are we better than that? What is the point of making these claims if they do in fact stand in opposition to our acknowledged ideals? This is the great failure of capitalism.

Threatening a person's ability to be financially successful or promising financial security are powerful motivators. In capitalism it is done subversively, almost making the victim seem responsible. In an oppressive state it's clear that the oppressor is causing the suffering. In capitalism though, we manipulate it so that it looks like these "failures" are unable to provide like a hard working person should be able to. When the truth is that the system has been designed to create "losers" and we are encouraged to blame these "losers". This creates the wanted schism and it further reinforces the belief of our own self-worth based on our own success. The old fear created by religious belief of deity-chosen leadership has very effectively been converted into this new scheme where the proletariat are set against each other by their very own ideas of self-worth.

The benefits of competition are actually highly overrated. The paradox is that in an attempt to make an organization more successful, internal competition actually creates destructive divisiveness. For example: The CEO of company A wants to increase sales, so she sets up a competition among its salespeople Pete, Debbie, and Katie. Pete takes a call from a potential client, but the client says she wants to deal with Debbie since they already spoke. How inclined is Pete to give Debbie the message? He is likely to write down nothing in the hope that the client will not call back. This is because he cares less about the overall business success than he does about ensuring his own advantage over other agents. The larger the financial worth of this potential transaction, the more inclined Pete is to sabotage Debbie, since it would greatly increase her chances of winning. By sabotaging Debbie he hurts the company too, but it serves his interest in winning the individual reward. There is also the potential that he will make an offer that is less profitable for himself or possibly even for the company, just to entice the customer to deal with him. Katie is not likely to speak well of any of her colleagues-turned-competitors to prospective clients. She may even make disparaging comments, making the whole group look bad and thus jeopardizing future business interests. The more lucrative and coveted the prize for winning, the more of this behavior will occur. It will create a divisive atmosphere of mistrust and potentially damage overall business by exposing potential clients to this dysfunctional internal relationship. If the prize is a pat on the back, it is likely to have no effect at all from a lack of proper motivation. No matter what the CEO says, it will be counterproductive. If she tells everyone how important it is to win, she will be encouraging the damaging behavior. If she tells everyone winning is not as important as being a team, she contradicts the point of the competition in the first place.

In contrast, if she makes the competition external in nature it will have the desired result. If the top three competing companies in their market average $50,000 of monthly sales, she should promise a prize to be awarded to the whole team if they beat that. Now Pete, Debbie, and Katie will work in conjunction. Speaking ill of co-coworkers to potential clients will only reflect badly on the whole company. Pete would be hurting his own chances of success by "losing" Debbie's message. With this externally focused competition, Pete will actually do everything he can to help Debbie with this deal. Making deals that are financially damaging to the company would be illogical. By working synergistically, they create a greater probability that the company as a whole will be much more successful.

This has been observed in many different business settings. In factories where there are multiple shifts, competitions have been initiated and the result has been decreased efficiency. Upon subsequent scrutiny, it was discovered that shifts would not do anything to help out the next shift. Sometimes they would intentionally leave a mess. Shift managers would not pass on relevant information and sometimes would go so far as to ensure that shortages manifested themselves on the other shifts. Workers focused only on the effectiveness of their own shift. Once the competition was shifted externally, shifts would then make sure the next shift was set up properly. Managers would provide detailed handoff reports and address concerns before they became issues, regardless of which shift it occurred on. The result was that the whole factory increased its efficiency.

So the advantages of a competitive environment are not wholly true. Yet, it is the lie that we have been convinced of, because it serves to set us against each other. Capitalism is reliant on the adversarial relationship amongst the laboring segment. How better to achieve this, than to convince the working segment that it is advantageous to compete against one another? As workers strive to outmaneuver each other, they generate greater wealth for the one percent and the only cost is the diminished welfare of other workers. In other words, the one percent gains at no cost to them. We in turn continue to compete for a greater portion of the same slice of pie. In our ignorance, we revel in our increased portion of the same crumbs. We ignore that we are only taking from each other, rather than doing what we should; take the whole pie and divvy that up amongst everyone.

The most common argument to justify competition is that if "Someone wants to do better they should just work harder or get a better job". This is a lie though. Capitalism is designed so that a majority of the population has to, by necessity, have a poor paying job that keeps them financially insecure. If literally everyone had the exact same possibility to better themselves, then theoretically everyone could be a billionaire, correct? So everyone who is not a billionaire is just lazy, right? Could this possibly work? Why would Warren Buffet work in Bill Gates' factory? There must be workers, meaning financially unstable people. There needs to be significantly more workers than owners, executives, and supervisors. It is critical to understand that capitalism NECESSITATES that a MAJORITY of the population be financially unstable. Everyone does not have an equal opportunity, because the system is rigged to guarantee that the majority will never attain financial security. Because if they did, who would actually labor and suffer in a capitalist economy? This is key to understanding the fallacy of the competitive argument in support of capitalism.

I agree that celebrating "graduation" from every grade in school and everybody getting a participation prize, can be detrimental to competitiveness and the inner drive to succeed or sometimes even to survive. I believe in hardship in training and being forced to overcome adversity. These are valuable lessons I learned and believe for my own kids. Many believe one of the greatest effects of capitalism is this very thing. That the enticement of great reward automatically motivates people to do better, to be better in fact. By removing all safety nets we increase the desire to succeed because now people realize that if they do not work hard and make money, there are no alternatives. The desire to eat and survive pushes us to be the best. Right?

Incorrect. Isn't one of the biggest complaints of professional sports, that they do it for the money and not the love of the game? This is one reason why college sports continues to be as popular today as it is. Not surprisingly, this popularity has infected college sports with the capitalist mentality and now it too is increasingly about the money. It is not long before the *reward* becomes the motivation and thus the original goal of instilling the drive to succeed is no longer the actual result. So now you have people who are highly motivated, but it is directly proportional to the level of reward that is offered. So you've created a dog. Congratulations. Because I can use the exact same methodology in training my dog and get a highly "motivated" dog. We should be aspiring to instilling the drive to succeed for the purpose of being morally upstanding people, not for the mere pursuit of financial reward. If you reward a child for good grades with candy, but neglect to intellectualize the importance of education and learning, then the child's only value system in this regard is candy. The act of learning has no value and if candy is removed, so is the only impetus to learn.

When talking about competition in this regard we must remember that we're not talking about a potato sack race. We're talking about people's welfare and their ability to live a fruitful and prosperous life. The truth is that for every snide remark you might think of to refute this belief of equity, someone richer than you could (and probably is) saying the same thing about why you don't deserve any more either. Competition and success can be good ideals that do make us better. But we need to define better. Does being a CEO making $20 million a year and employing people for $18,000 a year make you better? Is this really our litmus test for "better"? Is God really going to be happy when I say "Well Lord, I did what you wanted. I made other people tougher, by making them earn what they got. For their own benefit. To make them better. You know, the whole motivation to succeed thing, right?"

Now one might argue that if everyone is equal in AISE then why wouldn't everyone just be lazy in that system too? This takes us right back to the oversimplified and impossible scenario we've been convinced of. Yes, everyone in AISE is equal and their needs are equitably addressed. The difference is that, we democratically determine how much we need to produce and therefore how much we need to labor. Since there is no need for extraneous profit creation, there is no unemployment, and no theoretical wealth creators, we have plenty of labor. We all need to labor, because that is how we get what we want, just like now. But there are no "social" programs because everyone will labor in one way or another. I'll drill deeper into this in a later chapter, but please understand that this is not a common problem between capitalism and AISE.

Yet another form of conflict that the one percent utilizes is the misunderstanding regarding crime and criminal behavior. I'm not referring to crimes of sexual abuse, violence, or other despicable acts. I'm referring to crime as it relates to one person's attempt to reverse their socioeconomic disadvantage. In *Utopia*, Raphael Hythloday makes a poignant point when he makes the argument that executing thieves is a most ineffective way of discouraging theft. He is right to point out that for an extended period of human history, the economics of various cultures made it so that peasants were forced to steal for lack of any other options and then once they did, they were then accused of "being" thieves. As if it was some genetic predisposition that was the genesis of the theft. Rather than a socially created oppression that created the circumstances that left little choice. For a long time the allegedly educated and elite believed that criminals were people of a felonious mindset and that it was a behavior that needed to be stamped out. Now I am a huge proponent for taking responsibility for one's own choices in life, but when those choices are reduced to starving or stealing and nothing in between- that is not really a choice. There is certainly a big difference between a person born into poverty and some person who has irresponsibly gambled away their house and savings. I am not excusing irresponsible behavior. I am pointing out that capitalism creates the "have nots" and then we blame them for being "have nots".

Without the lure of outlandish financial gain or even just elevating one's financial status, what motivation is there for a lot of crime? Sure, junkies are still going to want their drugs and rapists are still going to want to rape, but what motivation would traffickers (of people or drugs) have? Right now the obscene amount of wealth to be gained offsets the risk of jail. This is the main impetus for trafficking, embezzling, and fencing. For those in poverty, even small increases in financial gain become worth the risk of jail, because what other options do many of them have? Isn't the explanation for the crime rate often the fact that a lot of these people suffer from socio-economic disadvantage? If you eliminate the capitalist aspect, why would one risk jail?

As long as you legally participate in the Altruistically Inspired Societal Economic system you will be totally provided for. What would maintain the current massive criminal enterprise if the risk of jail is now offset by the prospect of losing the already guaranteed prosperity? The argument has already been made to simply legalize drugs, as a misplaced solution. That's a great idea, because vices have never been exploited by mega corporations to make enormous profits...except for cigarettes...and alcohol...and pharmaceuticals. How long do you really suppose it will take for some corporation to step in and start producing marijuana more efficiently and take over the market? Right now they are waiting to see if the legality will hold up before making the financial commitment, but if they see a profit to be made you can be assured that they will. These flourishing privately owned businesses that make the legalization argument more palatable, will not last.

When the criminal element, which was profiting off this endeavor, is now displaced by more rich people getting richer, they're just going to do what? We haven't provided any alternative for them, so what will they do? Apply for unemployment? Stop putting it off and go back to get that college degree finally? No, they're going to do what they have to, which is either find another criminal enterprise, or we're going to suffer a wave of burglaries and robberies unseen before, because they have no other options. But by simultaneously removing the motivation for crime and providing a means for them to live a meaningful life, we create a more viable solution. How is removing this barrier and the capitalist motivation for crime not the right solution? Crime is not the problem. Many of these people are not motivated by crime. They're motivated by a will to live. Crime simply presents itself as the most viable option for them to live any meaningful existence. When we learn to accept our own culpability in these circumstances, in that by supporting capitalism we support a system that intentionally ensures that these people will be left with meager means of existence, then we can actually initiate real change. Capitalism begets crime. Don't point at capitalist countries with massive socialist programs in place, look at this country for the truth of this.

I am by no means excusing criminal behavior, particularly violent or sexual crimes. These people should be incarcerated regardless of the economic system in place. Consider this though. A common argument people make with regard to criminals is that, they wouldn't need to steal if they just got a damn job. For simplicity let us assume that half of the roughly 3.5% of the American population under correctional control (incarceration, probation, or parole) did just decide to get a damn job instead of committing criminal acts. Considering that the unemployment rate is currently around 8% what is this additional 1.75% of the population supposed to do, other than to bring that figure up to 9.75%? The reality is that if this was the case, there would also subsequently be many other people unemployed too, due to a lack of necessity (police, correctional officers, support staffs for correctional facilities, etc.). So even if these people committed to this common capitalist rhetoric, the likely effect would just be 11% unemployment.

I'm certainly not making an idiotic justification for crime. I am not suggesting that we accept, or even worse, promote crime to stave off higher unemployment numbers. I agree that the malingerers and lazy people should have jobs and that criminals should be in jail. My point is that how are these people supposed to resolve their financial difficulties by simply getting a job, if 8% of the population already can't? Far more than 8% of the population actually has no employment and even more lack full time employment. These facts are conveniently and intentionally hidden in the criteria for developing the statistical data. The truth is that if they all actually did seek employment that would not solve society's problems as we have been led to believe. If you think I am mistaken, then explain how if there is 8% unemployment already how adding another 3%, or more, of the population to the group of job seekers is supposed to solve that problem. It would only exacerbate the problem. We have convinced ourselves of the simplicity of the plight of these people, without considering the reality of the system which intentionally creates their situation in the first place. This is another example of how the one percent has convinced us to blame each other, rather than us realizing the failing of the system.

It's not about the absence of crime, hate, or mean words. Crime will still happen, jails will still be needed, but will there be anywhere near the same motivation for crime as there is currently? Why in the world would I sell drugs and risk jail if I can work on a farm, with the guarantee that my family's needs will be taken care of? Do we really believe that people want to be drug dealers, pimps, sex slave traffickers, and prostitutes? It's not the title and it certainly isn't the glamour of the occupations. It's because they know they don't have any other options and this is the quickest, if not the only way, for them to realize the American Dream of financial security. Everyone in AISE is not only guaranteed a job, but required to have one. A far cry from the current 8% unemployment rate we tolerate now. Think about that, at least 8% of our population that needs and *wants* a job, but for which there is no job available to them.

While classical economists thought that full employment could be maintained, Keynes correctly realized that this was likely to only happen if all necessary facets were in perfect alignment. Consider that at the height of WW II, the unemployment rate in this country was still 1.2% in 1944 and 1.9% in 1945. The fate of the world in the balance and victory by no means guaranteed in 1944 and yet we can't find work for 1.2% of the population that *wants* a job? We acknowledge and accept that 100% employment is basically impossible; in an economic system which strenuously advocates that everyone is to be responsible for themselves. If you want to succeed, the answer is no more complicated than: Get a job dammit. We are going to firmly and indignantly tell you it is your fault for being unemployed. Even though we know full well that the system we cling to and love is designed so that at least some of us will always be unemployed. The most likely way for you to change that is by someone else becoming unemployed. There is almost always going to be at least 2 – 3% of the people unemployed. So the only way for you to join the 97% of the employed, someone else must mathematically become part of the unemployed. Yet another way that the one percent manage to facilitate conflict among the working segment. If we can't get 100% employment in the middle of WORLD WAR II, then explain how we can tell poor people that the solution to their complaining is to simply get a job?

If 50 kids are playing musical chairs and there are only 46 chairs, would you berate and belittle the four kids left without a chair? It is not their fault. Four kids have to lose out every time. Have to. This is our economic system. Some people are going to be unable to provide for themselves basically at any given time, because it does not support 100% employment. What is our solution? "Be a winner". "If you were good enough you would have a job". "This is good, because it weens out the weak". Just one problem with this thought process. Suppose the four "weak" kids are allowed to die off. That doesn't mean that everyone now has a chair. It means the loss of those four will create diminished demand, which in turn means supply needs to be curtailed, which means not as much labor is needed. So now we have 46 kids but only 42 chairs. Again, four have no chair through no fault of their own. How many "weak" ones do we let die, as we thump our chests and proclaim how great we are for getting rid of the weak? At some point 100% employment is likely possible in capitalism, but with around 320 million Americans, just how many should we let die off before we agree that the ones remaining are "tough enough" to deserve to live?

I now realize that standing before God, telling him how proud I am of myself for being tough enough to help ween out the weak ones, is not what He is going to want to hear. Whatever your spiritual beliefs are, do you think this ideal is what you should be supporting? I believe in being tough and withstanding adversity, without a doubt. But watching a person starve to death, not for lack of desire, but for lack of the existence of a job is not being tough. That's just being despicable. As a Christian I can no longer look with favor upon this economic system we glorify and give praise to. Capitalism is the embodiment of callousness and depravity. Whether you pray to God, Allah, Buddha, or no one, is this really the spiritual path you believe you should be on?

Marx and Engels correctly identify the need for capitalism to constantly reimagine the forms of production and thus the relations to that production. It must forever change and find new markets and new items to consume. Very prophetic when you consider the current situation. Capitalism must be in a constant cycle of expansion into new markets to continue to function. Stagnation is one of the greatest threats to capitalism. If there is no new technology, service, gadget, or what-have-you then the whole system deflates as production dwindles down due to a saturation of goods and services. Prices then drop too. As prices drop so do wages and eventually rates of profitability decrease too. Notice I said rates of profitability. Production and sales will continue to make profit or they will cease to occur. But because there is no great demand any more, the profitability rate decreases until it is just profitable enough to justify the action of production and sales, but not much more than that. This is why new products must be introduced to the market at regular intervals. These must be met with great fanfare and anticipation so that there are high levels of sales.

The development of the wool industry in the 18th century is a good example of the effect of new markets, as it caused a shift in labor needs. There had been a need for a large workforce to farm the land, but only a handful of shepherds were now needed to tend to flocks of sheep grazing on the vast areas of land. This displaced workers and also caused grain prices to spike. This was due to less grain being produced from less land being dedicated to grain production. Even wool prices increased from the inability to meet the continually rising demand for more wool. We see this repeatedly, as markets disappear due to advancement. The advancement is good. The impending financial collapse for those involved is not. One industry becomes obsolete, thereby triggering massive unemployment and displacement. Sometimes it's as simple as a single factory shutting down and wreaking economic havoc over an entire populace. The ramifications of this can last for generations. Everyone is familiar with this scenario and everyone laments the effects of it, but most are unwilling to acknowledge that it is the intrinsic instability of capitalism which is the very cause of this.

The problem is that there are a ton off excuses and explanations that can, and are, made. Some will say, "Well these people should just move, get new training, or get a new career." Others will go so far as blame these people for not being smart enough to get into a better career from the beginning. Yet, at some point this factory or industry was gainfully employing people and according to the standards of capitalism it was right that these people filled these positions. Even right up to the very end of the lifecycle of the factory or industry in question. It would actually have gone against the very principles of capitalism for workers not to continue working. That would defy the supply and demand theory. I'm not arguing against the logic of getting off the sinking ship, but within the confines of the logic of capitalism, people should not leave these jobs prior to them being dissolved. Being dismissive towards people's financial plight, which is artificially generated by the economic contrivances that we have built, does not seem to be particularly humanitarian to me.

We need to understand that capitalism fosters and depends upon this constant upheaval. Every time workers are forced to seek out a new means of subsistence, it fosters conflict amongst them. Those who choose to remain in the old industry will accept massive declines in pay and benefits, happy just to have a job. Those who move on will meet fierce competition from others who are similarly displaced and thus they will all be tempted to accept whatever benefits and pay are offered for fear of being left without a job altogether. Both these scenarios benefit the one percent as the workers are pitted against each other in competition to fill a limited number of positions.

What is Your Motivation?

I am only one, but I am one. I cannot do everything, but I can do something. And I will not let what I cannot do interfere with what I can do.

Edward Everett Hale

Allegedly in AISE there will be a lack of motivation to be successful because there will be no lure of financial gain. I suppose we need to first define what "successful" means. We associate higher education with the positive attribute of desiring to provide better for one's family or self. This is lauded as an admirable trait and certainly it is commendable in that respect. Doing so typically requires one to spend less time with one's family, friends, or community since great amounts of time and effort must be devoted to school work. This in turn usually leads to a job that while having higher financial rewards, requires greater amounts of time and focus. Again, this results in diminished time to spend with one's family, friends, or community. While I'm certainly not insinuating that higher education is not positive or useful, I am questioning its direct association with "success". The successful chef/novelist/business owner/whatever who tirelessly works 20 hour days is usually spoken of in a positive manner. Once more, this is admirable in the desire to make oneself better and to improve one's situation. But how easy is it to forget that the original intent of such focus was to be a better provider for one's family or self? Or perhaps to provide the means to travel or finance specific hobbies. Or to be good at a job that has a positive social impact. Sadly the main motivation in this country has recently shifted from higher ideals to that of simple money making. This likely has a lot to do with people wanting more wealth so they can achieve financial security, which is increasingly difficult to do. One could argue that this motivation to make money is based on a desire to obtain security. In AISE one does need to worry about providing individual security. The wealth and luxury of the society is equitably distributed. This is how the shift is made. Instead of individual wealth accumulation being the motivator, the motivator is that when we all labor, we all prosper.

It is often argued that without the motivation of profit there will be no incentive for advancement. So no one currently working towards a cure for cancer gives a damn about cancer patients? If they could make the same or even more money making piñatas, they would drop everything and head to the piñata shop to get a job? Are we so jaded that we believe that no one would want to find a cure for cancer unless there was a substantial bonus attached to it? Much undo credit is attributed to capitalism and it is often held on a pedestal for the technological advancements that we have today. As if the evolutionary development of capitalism suddenly and solely gave rise to these great advances. While it is true that profitability has become the focal point for modern scientific advancement, this can hardly be applied in a historical context. This current development should come as no surprise, given the highly prevalent focus on greed and personal interest today. It is a cultural mindset though and those can be changed if there is a desire to do so. Just as a cultural shift allowed this to become true, another cultural shift can allow us to adopt Altruistically Inspired Societal Economics.

In general, crediting the advancement of technological developments to any singular source is impossible. There are too many facets to consider. One can easily argue that the ancient inventors had a much more daunting task because they had less to build off. Modern inventors have the luxury of referencing the findings and failures of those before them. The number of inventors more recently can also be ascribed to better education systems and the luxury of time that previous developments have created. The simple act of taking a bath used to require getting buckets of water, gathering wood, building a fire, heating the water, then transferring the hot water to the tub. Now one turns a knob. The average person lives a less arduous life and can therefore spend more time pursuing intellectual endeavors...or playing Angry Birds. There is no evidence to assert that profit and wealth were the motivation for the scientific exploration of Leonardo da Vinci, Galileo, or Archimedes. Yet they stand among the most celebrated inventors. They sought to advance human knowledge and experience, because they could. We have been taught to forget that people used to strive for loftier goals than just wealth.

The military and NASA are directly responsible for the development of the internet, early computers, rocket technology, aerospace development, many medical discoveries, and more. Whether these programs were conducted by military personnel or merely funded by them is irrelevant, since in most of these cases the government owned the rights to any developments. These were people who chose to work for the advancement and protection of society, because they believed in it. Working for the government or a government funded project typically comes with publicity restraints as well as minimal financial rewards. A lot of this technology, which current advancements are based on, are due to the efforts of people with no expectation of receiving great wealth. Typically, the modern response to this is to call these people foolish. I applaud these people for their dedication to the belief that they were serving society with their intellect, rather than feeding self-serving interests. This serves as recent evidence that profit is not the only incentive for scientific advancement.

Many defense contracts fall into a quasi-socialist category as well. I would not argue that defense contracts are indeed highly lucrative for the individual companies, but it is not a true application of capitalism either. The government agrees to pay these companies to research certain types of technology, which serves to eliminate the high risk usually associated with research and development. Much of this technology would never be developed in true capitalism, due to the high risk of failure and for a lack of marketability in the short term. It is really only due to the government subsidizing the R&D costs and guaranteeing a market for the completed project through the allocation of wealth collected from the masses. This is not capitalism promoting technological advancement, but altruistic motivation.

Suffice to say that neither the pace nor the scope of technological development can be singularly attributed to either economic function. Both AISE principles and capitalist influences have had an effect on the advancement of science. More to the point though, it is baseless to make the assertion that scientific advancement would somehow stagnate as a direct result of removing capitalist influences. People refuse to believe that it is possible to motivate human greatness by a means other than fiscal reward, whether it be currency or physical possession of a valued good. Now the primary assumption here is that, regardless of the economic system in play, that personal gain is defined as not just some form of substantive recompense, but the primary motivator. Other intangible motivating factors are not considered relevant, since the assumption is that they are not sufficient enough to motivate people to achieve more. Without the promise or at least expectation of increased personal financial gain, people would be content to merely muddle along at the status quo. This of course is the supposition of people who have been raised in a monetary based capitalist society from their earliest memories and have known nothing else. How then do we explain, soldiers, relief workers, acts of charity, paramedics, foster parents and a litany of other selfless professions and deeds that actually defy the capitalist ideals? The fact is that despite misanthropic misgivings about humanity, there are clear examples of people acting in total disregard of financial reward.

We have already explored the alleged "human nature" to be greedy, to be selfish, or to consume voraciously and devoid of reasonable constraint. Are we human beings with intellect and God-given ability to think and choose? Or are we no more than a dog that responds to nothing but instinctual, chemical driven responses? I for one cannot fathom a world in which I am no more than the sum of random chemical parts. We have been conditioned to believe that money is and should be our main motivator. This is because the more we become dependent on our jobs as a means to achieve the promised financial gain, the easier we are to manipulate.

When a musician achieves commercial success, aren't they often immediately derided for "selling out"? For giving into the pop music success rather than being true to the music? The aloof attitude toward indie films is similar in that there is an assumption of artistic integrity over the monetary success that blockbuster movies generate. As if the two elements are somehow opposites and impossible to embody simultaneously. Don't we favor the athletes that play "for the love of the game"? Don't we boo and disown those who turn their backs on the franchise that found them, to pursue big money free agency? Don't many fans complain that financial success often hurts performance? We recognize those who produce or work for more than just a paycheck. We appreciate them for their exuberance and passion for what they do, rather than the hired mercenaries. This is one reason why Derek Jeter is revered, while people have no hesitation to turn on A Rod. Yet at the same time we have grown to excuse such profiteering behavior, because it is smart business. In our own desire for financial security we realize that we too would demand $20 million a year if we could throw 55 touchdowns in a season. We have sheepishly accepted that this is the way of the world. But we know that this is not true. We know that many athletes, artists, chefs, teachers, firefighters, and many other people do what they do because they are passionate. That not only would these people continue to do the best that they could in these fields, but that we would love them even more for it. Ask yourself what you would passionately pursue if not constrained by the need to provide, financially. We forget that not so long ago people actually did things for the love of it or for the simple desire to be great. Despite what we might be inundated with today, it *is* conceivable to live in a world where people are actually motivated to do great things- without the sole lure of money.

Life is about perspective. How we see things as individuals and our opinions on how we believe that others see things. It is something that people in general struggle with. It is only exacerbated by the fact that greed and self-reliance is the core of capitalism, which currently is deeply intertwined within American culture. It makes seeing and understanding other perspectives difficult. An inability to see issues from other perspectives fosters distrust and hate. It is essential for us to be able to see the possibilities that exist beyond our current state. To do so requires being able to see matters from different perspectives than we are currently accustomed to. We must be able to see a world that is not corrupted by capitalism and where people are not purely financially motivated.

Here is my best example of perspective. If you know how the refraction of light affects a spoon in a glass of water, try to remember how you felt when you saw it for the first time. If you are unfamiliar with this, then try it out. Imagine a smooth, clear glass that is half filled with water and has a regular size spoon in it. The glass is put in the middle of a large round table. Then picture that table with 12 strangers standing around it looking at the glass. Except for one person who is only looking at the glass from eye level. All of them may only observe the glass from their own position. No person is allowed to shift their view point. They are only allowed to look at the glass from their initial viewpoint and straight on from their place at the table. Each person then describes what they see. Some of the people will say that they simply see a smooth, clear glass that is half filled with water and has a regular size spoon in it.

However, a few or perhaps only the one person viewing at eye level, will describe a smooth, clear glass that is half filled with water, but the regular size spoon is transected and the two halves are offset from each other. If the 12 people are unaware of the affect that the refraction of light has on the spoon, they will be unable to explain anything other than what they see. As a person, not knowledgeable about light refraction and looking at the exact same glass of water just a few feet away, it would be easy to assume this stranger was either lying or crazy. Particularly since a majority of the other strangers would agree that there is no such transection taking place. This is the prime example of how, many different people can look at the exact same item (or theoretical issue) and see something uniquely different.

If two of the people with differing descriptions were allowed to switch places and see the glass from the new perspective, they would then quickly be in agreement with each other and have newfound trust and respect for each other. This comes from being able to see the same object now from two different perspectives. Neither of them has to imagine or visualize what the other is saying, but now they have actually experienced it. The power of seeing the same issue from a different perspective cannot be overstated. It's easy to make generalizations and assumptions about a group without really understanding them and what they go through. It is intriguing how it is so common for people to insist how they are the exception to the rule, yet the same people are usually quick to apply that same rule indiscriminately upon everyone else.

The strangers who do not switch places have a few choices. They can choose to believe that it is possible that these other people do in fact see something different, whether it be real or an illusion. The main point is that they believe the others to be mentally sound. This represents a willingness to discuss issues openly, with the possibility of being persuaded to change their own opinions or to accept new ideas. It means they are willing to accept that there are alternative perspectives that have substance and that the possibility exists that they may even be mistaken. They can believe whole heartedly that the spoon has in fact been transected based purely on the verbal testimony of the others. This demonstrates a great deal of faith in the others' perspective. This is perhaps the most powerful choice, in that it necessitates a true leap of faith. To realistically see and value an issue from a point of view one has never personally experienced is special. The strangers can also choose to believe that the others are liars or crazy. From there they can, at best, feel pity for the apparent lack of mental capacity of the others. At worst, they will hate the others because they think they are insane or dishonest.

There is no scientific evidence that humans naturally lack morals and even though Christianity acknowledges that we are sinful in nature, it makes no claim that humans are incapable of morality. The problem is that we believe what we see. When we see it often enough we make the irrational conclusion that this means that this is "normal", "natural", or that it therefore can be applied universally. This is not science. I recently read a social media comment where someone claimed that he "intelligently applies common sense and makes judgements based on what I see." Isn't this exactly the kind of ignorance that the scientific community had to overcome to be recognized as a legitimate source of knowledge? I cannot see oxygen molecules, therefore they do not exist, right? Have we really devolved? No, we simply need to change our perspective and understand that it is absolutely possible for us to change our motivations from selfish to altruistic. There is strong evidence that this is already the case, but that the circumstances created by capitalism block its effective development.

As a nation, the issues of starvation and poverty could be addressed correctly and these problems solved. The problem does not lie in a lack of net worth, but in the disproportionate distribution of that net worth. It's easy to lay blame on poor people for not spending properly or as we've talked about before, blaming them for their station in life. We have been conditioned to automatically assume that if a person is poor that it is because they have not tried hard enough. Is this really any different from thinking that being a criminal is somehow genetically linked? I'm not suggesting that we eliminate personal responsibility, far from it. What I am suggesting is that we see things more clearly from differing perspectives. We, as a society, can alter our cultural priorities from wealth accumulation to altruistic concern. It may not be a simple task, but it is possible. More importantly it is right.

Religion

*Do not go where the path may
lead, go instead where there is no
path and leave a trail.*

Ralph Waldo Emerson

The two most important decisions one can possibly make in life are those regarding religion and finances. Both of these decisions are inter-related. Sadly, most of us spend more time figuring out what we want to eat for lunch each day than we do cumulatively on either of those two decisions. Regarding religion, the rationale is that at the end of the day there is only one correct answer. Either there is God or there is not. Or we really do get reincarnated into a moth. Or there is nothing. Either the Catholic belief system is right or the Jehovah's Witnesses are correct. The point is that everybody's belief can't be right. If you're an atheist and the Methodists are right, that is going to be quite unfortunate for you. It is an important enough choice that it warrants serious consideration. So that you feel confident in the choice that you make. No one wants to find out they made the wrong choice when they die. Depending on your religious beliefs, your financial choices may also affect what happens to you in the afterlife. The financial choices that you make will impact your life in very poignant ways. If you have no money; vacations, entertaining gadgets, even medical procedures are going to be unavailable to you. The leading cause for divorce is financial stress. Eating healthy and living luxuriously can be expensive, and both of these factors could help you live a longer, more fulfilling life.

I am not thrilled with the current social belief that if you dare to open your mouth about something that one person in the world does not agree with, then you are "disrespecting" that person. At some point here we're going to be a planet of stagnant morons who only talk to each other about the weather for fear of "insulting" someone. We should be challenging conventions with open dialogue amongst respectful people seeking enlightenment. Unfortunately we see, on all sides, the prevalence of people who are quick to declare emotional injury. They profess to seek truth, but in actuality only desire the last word and righteous recognition of being deemed correct. As it is, we are forming little camps where we only express ideas with likeminded people. Like some weird intellectual incest because there is no evolution of these thoughts and nothing new is ever being added. It's just the same thought passed back and forth with a congratulatory and empowering "you're so right" each time.

I suppose progress has been made. We have evolved from discerning schism boundaries amongst humans from geography, to physical differences, to religious beliefs, to choices of intellectual ideals and views. The point here is that we need to start conversing and not just talking. That means listening and thoughtful consideration to what someone else says, to the same degree to which you demand regarding what you are saying. I hope to foster understanding from this perspective and engender some progressive thought. To at least start down the pathway to the next evolutionary epoch of this development of human division, where ultimately there is no more human division. I don't expect one to drop this book and burn all their money. I am not sure that AISE will even occur in my lifetime, but every change has to have a beginning. And if I can play a part in fostering that beginning, then I would be honored.

My reluctance in covering the religious aspect of this topic is based on the fact that this is a complex discussion already. Adding religion into it risks making it so convoluted as to lose any opportunity to initiate a change in anyone. However, the inspiration of this book stems directly from my religious values and beliefs. So I feel that there is no way for me to write this book without acknowledging that inspiration. If you are Christian I believe and hope that this chapter will have significant value for you. If you are not Christian I entreat you to read on if for no other reason than to gain understanding of my reasoning. I am not preaching, I am stating my beliefs, and I hope I am educating. All I can do is write what I feel is right, I cannot make you feel any particular way. Only you can determine your reaction to it.

I am confident in my religious beliefs as a Lutheran. I am unapologetically religious and regardless of anyone else's unfortunately negative experience or perception of the religion, mine has been positive and empowering for as long as I can remember. That being said, I do not believe that only Lutherans or even Christians have some exclusive ability to be empathetic, caring, or merciful. If anything, I am attempting to connect with those sentiments within you, whether you are agnostic, atheist, Buddhist, or whatever. It is emphatically not my contention that Christians have any kind of superior ethical or moral standing than anyone else. In fact my belief is that all of us are sinful and that no individual or group has any favoritism with God over anyone else. The difference lies in the belief of how we view the proper road to redemption and salvation. I believe that most religions teach positive and moral lessons, so this chapter should have relevance for most people.

There are those who believe that salvation can be achieved through good works in order to establish a greater number of good deeds to counteract the bad acts one has done. The final objective being to have performed more good than bad at the end of one's life. Others believe that karma works its way through the universe to create a balance of justice and good against bad. There are some who implement a code of honor which establishes the necessary parameters in judging right from wrong in the way one lives. Some believe that even though there is no higher importance to the distinction or pursuit of right versus wrong, they simply choose to do what is right because they have no personal desire to do harm to anyone else.

What I believe is that we are all sinful by nature and incapable of leading a "good" life or achieving greater levels of good than bad. I find it difficult to accept that there is a mathematical equation that calculates our sins and good deeds to determine whether we have achieved salvation or not. How can one really quantify the effect of being verbally vile to someone? I've been called a lot of bad things in my life and for the most part I haven't let it affect me. While I'll admit that I'm not generally sympathetic to someone who bursts into tears over being called a dummy (come on, sticks and stones), I also acknowledge that being mean to people can have devastating consequences. The point here is that this idea of living a "good" life can lead to focusing on keeping score, instead of just doing the right thing for the right reason. Are you really holding the door open for the old lady because you know it is good to do it, or is it because you know you lied to your wife this morning and need to start getting some wins to make up for it? As Lutherans, we believe that no one is beyond God's salvation and no sin is unforgivable by God, but salvation is not attained by leading a sinless life because that is impossible. This is where many people get lost though. They assume that since we believe that we are sinful and that it is futile to live a life of scorekeeping, that this means that we can now have a free for all.

> 1 What shall we say then? Shall we continue to sin, that grace may abound?
> 2 God forbid. How shall we, that are dead to sin, live any longer therein?

Romans 6:1-2

This verse says that we are not to just go ahead and sin as much as we want. We believe that by dying on the cross, Jesus Christ paid for all of our sins and thereby provided salvation for us through his own suffering. According to my understanding of Lutheranism, all that is required of us to receive this great gift is to believe that this is true and to repent for our sins. But Jesus' sacrifice was not intended as an all-encompassing get-out-of-jail-free card, so we could be free to sin as much as we want and then just say we're sorry for it at the end of the day. Being sorry and asking for forgiveness means being sorry and asking forgiveness for lacking the strength to not sin. I repent for lacking patience and yelling at my kid, I repent for not controlling my anger, etc. Sin may be inevitable, but that does not mean it is unavoidable. By this I mean we will sin more often than not, but that doesn't mean we are incapable of overcoming all temptations all the time. We can't live the "good" life as previously discussed, but we can try and do the best we can. That is what makes all the difference, trying.

This confuses some people. They mistakenly believe that this means that we believe that all we need to do is half-heartedly say "I'm sorry" and then we're good to sin again. I believe in an all-powerful God who knows everything and can do anything. Do you think that I believe that I can fake him out by pretending that I'm sorry? This is why it is not for anyone to tell anyone else whether they are going to Heaven or Hell. Only you know if you truly repent for the sins you have committed. Regardless of the outward behavior or affect that the rest of us see, no one can know your true intent and feeling except you and God. This is how I interpret that we are not to judge others. Only God is fit to judge who is truly repentant and will therefore go to Heaven. Not judging others also does not mean standing idly by and allowing unfettered access to fresh victims for rapists and pedophiles because we don't want to be "judgmental" of them. If anything, imprisoning them not only protects new innocents from suffering but also limits their ability to repeat that sin. It provides time for reflection, to hopefully lead these people to true repentance. More often than not we will fail at not sinning. That is the core of the issue. What is key though, is trying not to sin in the first place, recognizing when we do sin, and truly repenting for it after.

Capitalism is very much like the same unacceptable theory of deliberately sinning, with the intention of asking for forgiveness later on. This is true in that we justify producing as much gain or profit as possible and then rationalize it with the idea that we will make it right later on with charitable giving. Think about that for a minute. It's okay for us to charge a person for a good or service, regardless of the level of need for it by that person, and on top of it charge them extra so that we gain by it. So I'm going to exploit you for the sake of personal gain, but I'll make up for it later by donating to charities. Charities of my choosing. And when I feel like I have sufficient surplus. And when it is convenient for me. So I'll help you when it fits my schedule, not your need.

> *...And Jesus said unto her, Neither do I condemn thee: go, and sin no more.*

John 8:11

Jesus assures the woman that she is not condemned; that her sin is not cause for damnation or exclusion from Heaven. He says this, after having told her accusers that being sinful themselves, it is not their place to provide judgement on anyone else. Divine judgement is for God alone. Yet he does not just tell her this. He ends by directing her to "sin no more". In other words, our sins cannot keep us out of God's love, because of Jesus' sacrifice; but this does not mean that we are free to sin at will either.

Nor is it intended that we should enable others to sin. Buying drugs for the drug addict or providing the means for the malingerer to waste God's gifts in slothfulness are not acts of love. Those are actually sinful acts, because we are simply assisting these people in sinning. AISE gives us the means to present a situation wherein everyone has a real and equal chance to provide for themselves in a meaningful way and thus live as productive and happy a life as possible. If people choose to shun this opportunity, then that is literally their God given right to do so. By refusing to work for the bounty that the system would provide them, they are choosing to be lazy and wasteful. This is not behavior that should be supported secularly or religiously. So they will not reap any benefits of the system and that is their choice. This is exactly the same as the Christian ideal that Jesus made a tremendous sacrifice for us and all we need to do is choose to accept the salvation that is just waiting there for us. This is the major difference between AISE and the current pseudo-socialist capitalism we practice now. We currently support the deplorable behaviors at both ends of the spectrum: laziness in the acceptance of undeserved social program benefits and laziness in the entitlement of benefitting from the wealth created by other's labors. Our charge should be to provide the means to elevate everyone to levels of equality, not support behavior we believe to be disgraceful and morally wrong.

You need a blanket right now for the foster kid you took in. But unless you can pay me the $15 it "cost" me to make it, plus $5 more to make it profitable for me, you'll have to wait until enough other people buy an ample amount of blankets from me so that I feel financially secure enough to make a donation. Then I'll make a charitable donation to an organization, which will in turn take that money and buy blankets from someone else who sells blankets under the same profit-seeking pretense. Finally at that time you can provide the foster child with a blanket. Somehow we have become so spiritually lost that this actually makes sense to us. The problem is that within the confines of capitalism this does all make sense. After all it doesn't make sense for you to donate all your money and then become dependent upon the same convoluted mechanisms to assist you. So because we buy into capitalism this then is rational. The next logical question should be, why do we buy into capitalism? This next reading explains that we should not be accepting capitalism.

2 *Bear ye one another's burdens, and so fulfil the law of Christ.*

3 *For if man think himself to be something, when he is nothing, he decieveth himself.*

4 *But let every man prove his own work, and then shall he have rejoicing in himself alone, and not in another.*

5 *For every man shall bear his own burden.*

Galatians 6:2-5

We are all expected to support everyone else to the best of our ability, but at the same time each of us also has an expectation by God to carry our own burden and be responsible for ourselves. The beginning clearly contradicts the very basis of capitalism. It does not say, "Once your own survival and comfort has been securely established, go forth and give what is left over." Which, let's face it, most of us don't even come close to that, because it's not as if we clean out our 401k's and savings accounts or sell our DVD collections to feed the hungry. We're supposed to bear each other's burdens. We are supposed to either all be fat and satiated, all starving, or all just a little hungry together. Not 1% eating to excess, both in decadence and exuberance, while 70% eat comfortably but making sacrifices in quality and health, with both demographics bemoaning the failings of some man-made economic system (which both demographics support) causing the other 29% to scrape together a meager subsistence or to starve. Perhaps it's just me, but I don't comprehend how a person who believes in God can read verse 2 and then in any way, shape, or form explain how capitalism conforms to God's message to us. No matter your religion, or lack thereof, it cannot be difficult to see the hypocrisy and lack of compassion in the reality that capitalism creates.

Verses 3 and 4 say, do not falsely take pride in your station in life, when in fact it is only due to the labor and generosity of another that provides that station for you. Instead, make sure that you have done the best that you can and celebrate that. It doesn't say that everyone has to work to the exact same level. The paraplegic, the infant, 100 lb. adult, and the athletic adult are not expected to produce the same fruits from their labors. Equality of the effect of labor is not mentioned. It's only saying that each person needs to not lay back and rely on the bounty provided by others, but to also prove in their own works that they are producing what they can. Our society is big on comparisons and competitions. It's not worth doing if you're not keeping score, right? We have to know who won and who is better than whom. This is not about that. This is about each person performing to the highest level possible, based solely upon the individual gifts that God has bestowed upon each. The athletic person is supposed to lift more and hunt more. The only competition is supposed to be in the mirror. Are you doing the best good with the gifts God gave you? That is the only measurement of labor equality we are supposed to consider.

It is not the intention of this book to suggest that we should, as a society, ignore the realistic necessities of the flesh. Clearly we have physical needs and mental and emotional ones as well. A treasured keepsake, certain collectibles, even the possession of a pet can have undeniable effects on human wellbeing. These are not to be ignored completely, in favor of the spiritual considerations. Rather it is intended that we seek a harmonious marriage of both needs. Surely just as important as it is to feed and clothe ourselves, and as just mentioned, consider the emotional aspects as well, it is just as important to consider the spiritual concern. We need to stop thinking in such extremist terms, as it has become fashionable to do. Gone, it seems, are the days where one can suggest a course of action that reasonably addresses two points of view. We should neither sacrifice the spiritual desires of our hearts any more than we should relegate ourselves to joint starvation.

This not a blasphemous endeavor to create Heaven on Earth, as a means to create perfection and thus make God irrelevant in our own manmade perfection. Certainly not. But it is an exercise in the application of one of the greatest gifts in creation. We are made in God's image, not in some trivial and narcissistic physical respect, but in that we have the freedom of choice. What we choose to do with that gift makes all the difference. It is *the* difference. Will we choose to do the best that we can? Or wallow in our own despair and sin with neither thought nor concern? We know that perfection is unachievable by us and yet we must strive to do just that. It is the effort and not the result that we will be judged on. This stands in stark contrast and profane opposition to the mantra of capitalism, where only realized wealth procurement matters. One's efforts and ideals are valued as nothing, only the fruits of one's labors has any substantive value. People are mocked and ridiculed for being injudicious enough to hold ideals higher than fiscal advancement.

> *He that trusteth in his riches shall*
> *fall; but the righteous shall flourish*
> *as a branch.*

Proverbs 11:28

Utopia

Your silence gives consent.

Plato

One of the more common criticisms of theories like AISE is that it is nothing more than fanciful imagination and impossible to achieve. Of course the term Utopian comes up often too. Utopia is in fact nothing more than a fanciful imagination and impossible to achieve. I want to recognize and demonstrate how Utopia was never intended to be a blueprint for reality. It was written by a wealthy man who was closely tied to the desires of the king. I have a tremendous amount of respect for Thomas More and to this day vividly remember reading *A Man for All Seasons* for the first time. As devout as he unquestionably was, it is indisputable that his belief in secular values was every bit as profound. Being a member of the one percent, he wrote an intentionally buffoonish description of socialism to ensure that such thoughts would be rejected by anyone who read it. I don't believe his intentions to be nefarious or self-serving, but More clearly wanted the reader to shun even the idea of Utopia by the end of the book.

It was commonly believed and accepted that everything belonged to the king. One only owned what one did as a result of the generosity of the king and that it was his right to reclaim anything at any time. These are clearly ideas that are contrary to altruistic economic ideals. It is then logical for More, in service to his king, to write a work of fiction that makes an economy based on altruism appear undesirable. He chose devotion to his religious belief over the wishes of Henry VIII in the end, but during his life he was a loyal servant to his recognized king and believed in the laws of man on Earth. Part of a king's duty, allegedly, is to protect his subjects from the evils of too much wealth or freedom as they are neither morally nor intellectually capable of making good use of such luxury. More's motivation for writing the book in the way that he did is likely based on his support of this idea. More understood that socialism would bring greater levels of freedom, wealth, and leisure time for any populace. Therefore it is likely that he felt that by dissuading any from seeking altruistic principles in economics, he would be saving their souls from damnation.

People mistakenly make the same assumptions regarding Utopia as they do *Mein Kampf*. It has often erroneously been declared that *Mein Kampf* offers a unique insight to the inner workings of Hitler. He wrote that book while he was in jail, because he had just incited a failed rebellion. He wrote the book with the full intention of publishing it and the sole purpose of manipulating people's perception of him, so that he could once again rise to power. This was not some melancholy soul-searching exercise of a man having a mid-life crisis. Every word and phrase was carefully considered to elicit future support. To think that perhaps history's most skilled propagandist and politician would unwittingly write and distribute a book that focused more on revealing his personal truths, rather than craft the image, persona, and messages that he wanted conveyed, seems disingenuous at best.

The same is true of More in writing Utopia. This is not a representation of what he would consider to be perfect, but instead it is intentionally crafted in such a way as to dissuade others from seeking to achieve it themselves. The book is written with the expectation that it will be read and judged by those of similar cultural and religious beliefs as his. This is the cause for such useless assertions like insisting that households should trade family members to ensure that every house is uniformly represented. This is why every house and every city are to be identical. Of course the visceral reaction to such claims of necessity as this will be negative. Thus he surreptitiously begins to establish the desired negativity toward the concept of

Utopia. There is no rational explanation given for this absurd and arbitrary "necessity", because there is none and More knows it.

More does clearly address the issue of wrong doing in Utopia. That it is not, as is commonly and inaccurately portrayed, perfect. It is not perfect, because such a concept is ridiculous when speaking about humans- particularly for such a pious man as More. After all it would be sacrilege for him to conceive of, hope for, or pursue a perfect existence by man on Earth. In his estimation, Heaven is the only perfect existence and is only possibly through the grace of God. So even in More's somewhat satirical approach, he recognizes that there will be imperfections that need to be addressed. Utopians seek to establish peace through fear. A sign of the time in which the book is written to be sure. Intellectuals of that time did usually choose to employ a punitive philosophy as a deterrent to crime and other unwanted behavior. I'm not arguing with the philosophy actually, but conventional intellectuals typically seek to subdue immoral, sadistic, and inhuman behavior with philosophical solutions. So this is actually not as dysfunctional as it might seem today, given the prevailing attitudes at the time More wrote the book.

It must be noted that throughout the book, More makes up ludicrous names for his characters. For example, Hythloday means "peddler of nonsense". They are a play on words and often denote a sentiment of nonsense or fiction. As if with the introduction of each fictitious character or city name that it is an opportunity for More to remind the reader that it actually is fiction and that such concepts are indeed drivel and unachievable. I would agree, in so much as it is unattainable given the arbitrary and puritanical standards which he attributes to the Utopians.

He creates an idealistic description of an absolute abhorrence of war and yet they are concurrently described as being righteous and proficient at warfare. They are actually portrayed as quick to declare war in the case of a citizen being physically harmed and also in the less noble circumstance of an ally simply suffering a monetary injury. This is likely a reference to and perhaps a jab at the Pax Romana, wherein the Roman Empire was able to preside over a period of peace in excess of 200 years. This was due in large part to their philosophy, and strict execution of it, to exact excessive retribution to any who would foolishly attack a Roman citizen. While there are distinctive and undeniable benefits to the application of this mind set, the practical execution presents very obvious moral complications. It is necessary to apply this practice in a very Draconian and unrelenting style in order for it be effective. Every missed opportunity to enforce the philosophy creates doubt by enemies that one has the resolve to see it through. This is not exactly harmonious with the supposed pacifist attitude of the Utopians.

This probability is further hampered by a self-professed distaste of physical exertion by the Utopians. They are described as having a common interest in improving the intellectual aspects of their being above all other undertakings. This perfect combination of intellectual expansion as a lifestyle and contempt for physical labor, inexplicably does not hinder their ability to be masters of warfare and its execution. This passiveness and loathing of warfare on all levels, juxtaposed against this apparent excellence in implementation of it (for they are described as righteously having won every conflict) seems quite Utopian indeed. They are even described as being "fierce" in their application of war. The fierce, warrior, intellectual pacifists. Yeah, because that makes sense. This is not to say that one must be an ignorant, warmongering, bloodthirsty cretin to be effective in war either. Quite the opposite is often the truth, but they are described as having such a distaste for war that it is neither studied nor practiced unless needed. Army Green Berets are not couch potato pacifists in their down time. They are Green Berets *all* the time. This is not exclusive to war either. No human endeavor can be executed at such a level of proficiency and dominance, without concerted effort and dedication. Michael Jordan has indisputable physical gifts, but what elevated him to the level of greatness that he achieved, was his staunch commitment to perfecting his craft.

The book is full of contradictions. In one paragraph he describes total religious freedom, and then follows that by describing the utter alienation of anyone who doesn't believe in the value of a virtuous life and an eternal afterlife. So you can believe whatever you want so long as it is in agreement with what I say it must align with? Sounds an awful lot like the unbeatable, lethargic, pacifist, warrior bad asses. Even though it is supposedly idealistically accepting of all religions, atheism is forbidden. Utopia does not tolerate violence or even overzealous or insulting language toward opposing religions. This is despite the fact that in real life More totally supported execution for the crime of heresy. So it is yet another clear indicator that Utopia is nothing of the sort and that it is not the imagined world of perfection that More himself would approve of. It is a mere exercise in philosophical exploration and an opportunity to dissuade others from seeking an altruistic economy, although you can see the influences of More in Utopia in other ways. It is just another, older version of propaganda by the one percent to instill in us a pervasive and visceral negative reaction to just the thought of anything like Altruistically Inspired Societal Economics.

Not Possible

With courage you will dare to take risks, have the strength to be compassionate, and the wisdom to be humble. Courage is the foundation of integrity.

Mark Twain

"It's never been done before" is a popular rationale for dismissing the idea of AISE. We recognize the ignorance of those in history who thought they knew what was and wasn't possible based on their sensible observations. Of course the Earth is flat, one just needs to look to the horizon to understand that. Sailing to the horizon means one will fall off the Earth and so it is ludicrous to send an expedition to do so. Metal is heavy. If you throw a hammer in the water, it sinks. So making a boat out of metal is the dumbest thing possible. Who is the greater fool though? Those who had no historical references to demonstrate the folly of such thought and no scientific understanding? Or us, who have the benefit of both, yet still indignantly proclaim the ability to divine what is and is not possible based on simple observation, before applying concerted, intellectual exploration?

I seem to remember hearing about two crazy brothers who had this ridiculous idea about making a machine that could fly through the air. I mean how stupid an idea is that? Not only does everyone know it's impossible, but for crying out loud it's 1903. Even if such an unbelievable feat were possible, don't you think humans would have already done so by now? Then I heard about some box that can magically heat food with some invisible rays or something. For how many thousands of years have humans had to use fire to cook? Now all of the sudden I'm going to supposedly be able to cook food in a single minute. Idiotic. Next you're going to tell me I'll be able to make phone calls from a miniature computer I can hold in my hand. How many other examples do I need to provide, to demonstrate the categorical ignorance of the assertion that "it's never been done before" as any kind of valid argument? The only difference is that you can now stand, in hindsight, and say "of course those feats are all possible". Yet the reality is that no one knew for a fact that any of these things were truly impossible or not until someone tried. One could argue that these are all scientific based examples and so do not follow the same constraints of logic as a sociological advancement like AISE. I will not concede that opinion, but okay let's explore that.

Apparently there is some foolish notion going about that one should be presumed innocent until proven guilty. That's the most ridiculous concept ever. As if the word of a nobleman were not all the proof one needed to decide innocence or guilt. I'm supposed to take the word of some peasant woman over that of a land owning man? For thousands of years of human history it has been proven that if a man cannot prove his own innocence, then he is obviously guilty. But now these "progressive" thinkers want us to believe that we can just somehow alter our perception of things and adopt this new policy that is clearly wrong. Some other people have been saying that intellectual capacity is not determined by race. Can you imagine living in a world like these insane people propose? Imagine everyone being given equal consideration as to their intellectual ability? As if all the different races are somehow equally capable of cognitive thought. Next thing you know people will be saying that mixing races is okay.

How about the Code of Hammurabi and the Magna Carta? Or the Hippocratic Oath or the Protestant Reformation? These are all examples of social evolution that were utterly inconceivable of being accepted, much less practiced by the masses. Yet here we are. These are indisputable demonstrations that the cultural viewpoints of entire societies can be and have advanced. How about Martin Luther King Jr.? Gandhi? Despite the overwhelming widespread and deeply held preconceived notions of what was socially correct in all of these examples, somehow change was made. Scientifically there are undeniable and unavoidable barriers that cannot be changed. Sociologically speaking though, these limitations are all but non-existent and history proves as much.

Slavery existed for thousands of years as an acceptable part of social function. Of course it still exists today, but not as a socially acceptable practice. If you consider that it has only been considered widely socially unacceptable for a little over 150 years, compared to thousands of years of acceptability, the argument that AISE cannot possibly take hold because it's never been done, loses a lot of credibility. Since the abolition of slavery proves that the global society can accept a change to something that had been so acceptable for so long, then why isn't AISE possible? How long do you think generations of people of varying cultures lied to themselves that as long as we treat the slaves "nicer" that there's no problem in allowing that institution to prevail? Do you honestly think that you would be content to be a slave, as long your owner treated you "nicely"? Do you support the argument that if people were born slaves, then they wouldn't know any better and thus it is not the same thing? Consider that a similar argument could be made for your situation. For example: "You've never been outside the United States or made more than $30,000 a year, so you wouldn't know what you are missing." Using the same logic there's no need to allow you to experience either of those things.

Slavery and enslaving of others is not just acceptable in *Utopia*, it is a necessary facet of life. It is discussed not in the sense of having to defend it morally, but just as a matter of establishing order in its proper execution. Like having to address what traffic practices will need to be agreed upon in order to guarantee efficiency and avoid chaos. This is a clear indicator of the influence of socially acceptable behavior and its effect on what one deems to be a perfect society. Of course we look at this and are appalled that it is so seamlessly included in the supposedly perfect society. Our moral sensibilities immediately recognize this combination to be dichotomous. We openly recognize a very similar sentiment and one much more recent, in that this country was founded by slave owners who wanted greater freedom. One can only hope that at some point in the future, others will look on us and our socially acceptable behavior of needlessly tolerating poverty and suffering, in the same anachronistic lens that we view the practice of slavery in *Utopia* or in the past history of this country.

The fact is that at one point or another, the various cultures of the world made a decision to right the wrongs that they had ignored for so long. When will our society right the wrong that is capitalism? At some point you need to ask yourself if you want to be the same as one of those people who said, "Hey, I'm not the problem. I treat my slaves really well. If it wasn't for me they wouldn't be able to take care of themselves, so I'm doing them a favor." Or do you want to be one of the people who recognizes that true change is needed? Someone who says these PEOPLE deserve better than what we're doing right now. Through the generations of human existence it has been argued many times that the abolition of slavery would destroy the current economic structure and ending slavery would create chaos. That freeing slaves would result in too many people attempting to use limited resources. There were a plethora of excuses, which were all irrefutable, to explain how freeing slaves would be disastrous. Clearly these excuses were all baseless.

I understand that the Emancipation Proclamation was not implemented purely on a desire to free the slaves. There was a great deal of political influence and consideration of its effect on the war effort that served as motivation for its timing. This country had been dealing with the issue of whether or not to continue allowing slavery almost from the birth of the nation. Various states, at differing times adopted provisions abolishing slavery into their state constitutions. More abolitionist organizations began to form and gain notoriety. There are a litany of legal issues proposed, passed, or rejected regarding slavery and the admission of new states as either free or slave states from 1776 all the way until the Civil War. The 1850's mark the time at which the discussion became very heated though. In hindsight we can now see how much the debates between Lincoln and Stephen A. Douglas in particular will influence the eventual outcome.

It took over a hundred years from the Emancipation Proclamation to the Civil Rights Movement to finally correct the racial inequity in this country. Some would argue that there is still a lot left to be done. While I believe there are certainly still some issues, the solution lies in all sides looking toward the future rather than festering on the past. I have been called every Asian racial slur there is, starting at the age of four, so I feel that I can say with confidence that I have a good grasp of racism in this country. The point though, is that if people wait for the perfect plan and the perfect time for implementing meaningful social change, nothing would ever get done. That is not to say that mindlessly rushing into change for the sake of change is correct either. But there needs to be a balance between the two neurotic extremes. We, as a society, must formulate the best plan possible, be prepared for difficulties, be aware that flexibility and further change will likely be needed, and most importantly have the courage and conviction to know that this change is what we should be moving toward because it is right. This is not a new concept. This very thought process has been implemented by other societies in history and by this one as well. It is time for us to recognize that history will judge us for our decisions in the present. Just as we judge those who came before us. We have the ability and the choice to decide to start changing our mindset and seeking a more responsible way to care for each other.

The only social changes that are impossible are those that we stubbornly declare to be impossible. If we only pursued the endeavors that were clearly possible to us, we would still be living in the wilderness and throwing rocks at animals to hunt. The exact moment that we open our minds to a possibility, it becomes possible. This theory has been proven in modern business applications. In order to establish an effective safety culture for a work environment it has become understood that we must push the boundaries of our expectations. By that I mean that we have learned that we can no longer apply old conventions.

Let me elaborate. Company A sets the new objective to no more than 3 work related fatalities per year. If the current rate of occurrence is 5 per year and there are only 2 deaths the following year, then it is a great success. The problem though is that because 2 deaths falls within the parameters of no more than 3, there will be no motivation to make further changes. By their own thought process then Company A has effectively predetermined the probable height of their success. By sheer luck it may happen to occur that there are no fatalities the following year, but it will not be due to the implementation of any new policies which effectively lower the statistical likelihood of such an event. This means that they are as likely to continue experiencing 1-3 fatalities per year. This all stems from the mindset that since fatalities are considered a given and it is not realistic to completely eliminate them, that certain at-risk behavior is thus acceptable.

Yet when we challenge this convention by asserting an objective of zero injuries or fatalities, we push ourselves to the probability of achieving higher levels of success. Now we look at a work procedure and instead of accepting that it is "safe enough" to meet the standards, we look at it from every angle to squeeze every bit of risk out of the process as possible. As this mindset is applied universally through the business, the probability of a fatality decreases more and more. Even if it is only incrementally safer as each new process is implemented to increase safety, it makes it just that much more possible to achieve zero fatalities. We need to concede the reality that all human endeavors are destined to experience some deviation from perfection at some point, yet we still set the bar for perfection.

By taking on the mindset that no injury is acceptable we then create the highest probability of achieving the perfection we seek. Otherwise we limit or at least lower the probability of that success. This exact same mindset is applied to the elimination of manufacturing defects. By painstakingly poring over every manufacturing and product handling process, companies have achieved unheralded heights of quality control. These programs have fancy titles like Six Sigma and Lean Processes. The same can be said of the goal for implementing AISE. We will not all be healthy all the time. Shortages of natural resources, accidents, and even societal choices to accept certain risks will make it certain that there will always be those who must suffer, lose, or otherwise not be fully content. Yet if we commit ourselves to this goal of serving the best interests of society above and before all else, we stand the best chance of adopting an economic system that can provide for everyone in a moral and effective manner.

We can reflect on similar historical moments of profound sociological advancement. The Magna Carta went through a number of revisions. If one starts with the inception of the original written idea then its history can be traced back over the course of 300 years. The Bill of Rights were not ratified until 19 years after the Declaration of Independence and the 27th Amendment was just ratified in 1992. Yet these are improvements that were needed and were beneficial. Perfection is not, and likely never will present itself, just as it did not in these cases. We need to change our mindsets and start looking for the right answer. It is there, we simply need to commit ourselves to finding it. When JFK made his bold declaration that we would go to the moon, it was not an endeavor that we were even close to achieving at that time. In fact much of the technology that was necessary to do so, hadn't even been invented yet. That was going to the moon. Are you seriously going to tell me that it is impossible for a great society of people to commit to a spiritually superior path and find the necessary economic system to make it happen? In order for profound change like AISE to occur, there would need to be a significant alteration to the current social mindset, a visionary leader, and widespread legislative changes. It is feasible that our current capitalist system could be improved with truly fair socialist control methods and better wealth disbursement. This would only require a significant alteration to the current social mindset, a visionary leader, and widespread legislative changes. Sound familiar? So why not just make it right instead of doing all that just to make it "better"?

What is. What Could Be.

Alone we can do so little; together
we can do so much.

Hellen Keller

The whole point of AISE is that it is a system which will be governed and shaped by the democratic will of the people. Therefore the best I can do is offer an idea of what production choices are possible and which methods are probable. It is not the feared dictatorship or the vision of one particular person. No individual or small group of individuals can lay down a blueprint of what it will be, because that all depends upon the will of the people. One percent of the population cannot declare what and how things are to be made. That is the stuff of oppressive oligarchies, which is exactly what we suffer now. We cannot be afraid of progress because of the failures of the past. Isn't that one of the mantras that has served to make this country so great? We as Americans are never afraid to set the standard rather than meekly following it. If the current business model fails, we do not let that hinder us from finding the model that will succeed. Isn't this the entrepreneurial spirit that is supposed to make capitalism so great? Capitalism has failed us, both spiritually and for many of us physically too. It's time to exercise that entrepreneurial spirit we're so proud of and implement AISE.

A government would still be needed to implement AISE, but it would likely be smaller than it is now. Certainly we would still need federal authority for military protection and management, as well as for foreign trade and relations. There would be no need for the IRS though. It would be up to us to determine the extent of publicly operated companies versus government operated services. All companies would be publicly operated. Essentially they would become independent microcosms of a republic government, because society as a whole would own these companies. All decisions about the company would be driven by the CEO and board much like it is now. There would be two great differences though. First, profit and stock value would be non-existent and therefore would have no bearing on any decisions. Second, the executives of the company would be periodically elected democratically. These elections could be nationally or we could choose to make voting restricted to the locale in which the company is based. Each company could then maintain a certain element of individuality based on the leaders chosen. This is exactly how it is today, except that we would choose the leaders, not other members of the one percent. Also, the way for these leaders to keep their jobs would be by satisfying the wishes of the majority of the voters- the workers and consumers. Worker safety, environmental conservation, and product quality would become top priority in every choice.

By choosing to have companies that are independent of the government, we would further alleviate the potential for the nightmare oligarchy or fascist scenario. This is nothing more than one possible structure and a lot would rest in the hands of our society on how we choose to actually proceed. It is definitely more realistic to continue with the practice of a republic format as we already do, because of the sheer scale. The key is that without capitalist fiscal influence present to corrupt the system, it could operate equitably. The application of much needed term limits for all elected officials would ensure turnover so that no one could become as deeply ensconced as our current politicians and members of the one percent are.

People commonly ask, "Well what do you propose to do with people who refuse to put forth their best effort? Kick them out?" Well...yes. Why wouldn't that be the case? AISE is not a concept borne out of ignorant and fanciful daydreams of fairies and unicorns flying around. What do we currently do with people who disobey the requirements of capitalism? What do you call life without the possibility of parole at Ryker's Island? A sabbatical? An extended retreat? Robbers, burglars, tax evaders, embezzlers, and con artists are the labels we give to those who fail to comply with the regulations necessary for capitalism to function. Murder and rape would continue to be illegal and some methodology of controlling such behavior would be required just as it is today. Those caught malingering, stealing, misusing resources, or otherwise abusing the system would still need to be punished. This proposal has nothing to do with hugging rapists while singing kumbaya. It is not some fantasy where people joyously sing and dance while toiling at laborious work and others joyously sing and dance while relishing in obscene luxury.

The misplaced belief that AISE somehow translates into a vacuum of not just fiscal, but even moral responsibility, is a terrible hindrance to getting people to accept and understand the value of it. This is what pseudo-socialist capitalism is devolving into, but as I have hopefully made clear by now these are two separate systems. The malingerers and "professional entitlement seekers" cannot and will not be tolerated in AISE. Will it be perfection? No, of course not. If the standard for success is the absence of illegal activity, then defense of the current system has no leg to stand on. The standard for proposing change cannot be perfection. AISE will require laws and social value shifts that hold people accountable for their actions. For those who believe such social value shifts are impossible, consider that "separate but equal" was only just struck down in 1954. Women's suffrage only became legal in this country in 1920. These are just a few examples of social value shifts that were considered impossible too.

In AISE everybody is gainfully employed according to their ability. That simply means that just because you are blind, that does not mean there is nothing you can do to benefit society. Obviously driving a cab is a bad idea, but there are definitely meaningful occupations that are available. The reason 100% employment is possible is because there is no budget that artificially restrains the number of workers we can employ.

There is no breakeven point that we need to caution against rising above and losing profitability. Right now we have social workers and foster child case managers who are so inundated with work, that they are incapable of effectively performing their jobs. This is not for a lack of need for more employees, but because there is not enough money in the budget. Currently we have almost 8% of Americans that are unemployed and thus have no means to support themselves. Instead, we could be tasking them to perform work that is desperately needed and has great societal benefit. Further consider how many bankers, accountants, stockbrokers, insurance agents, marketing and advertising agents are currently employed with no other goal than to maximize profit and generate wealth. Since these positions would be unnecessary in AISE, they could all become available for other types work. There are currently labor shortages in critical positions that we lament, but tolerate or leave for volunteers to fill. So a possible "problem" we could run into is "too many" social workers. There is no reason to believe that we could not have many more hospitals or clinics. We could support and properly staff many more orphanages, "Make a Wish" affiliates, animal refuges, environmental restoration services, veteran care facilities, and many other types of community building programs. We will no longer have the failings of capitalism to deal with. There is no reason why we cannot all work more efficiently and less, while producing more.

In AISE the elimination of starvation and the provision for universal healthcare are addressed first. Then, since society is established in such a way that each person earns their equitable share of the goods and services provided, universities and colleges can be operated without needing to produce any profit or product other than learned graduates. The standards for admission and graduation can once again be based purely on one's ability, rather than being influenced by the business aspect. Anyone who had a desire and a reasonable ability to go to college, could.

Let us consider a current hot topic, free college for everyone. A number of groups are pushing heavily to provide free tuition for everyone. There are a few questions that need to be answered though. The most important one should be, how exactly are we going to pay for this? If we're going to hold on to this capitalist mentality and insist on adhering to this system, then where exactly do the funds come from? Are we really insisting that giving a young adult a free college degree is more important than feeding a 5 year old? Because that is exactly what we are saying. Every time someone clamors for free tuition for everyone and neglects to mention eradicating hunger in this country FIRST, then that is exactly what they are saying. Are we going to penalize the rich to pay for this? Why would you support that idea if you support capitalism? Where does it say "You are free to make as big a fortune as you can...until a point...and then we're going to penalize you"? That is never mentioned in capitalism. The American Dream is all about dreaming as big as possible. Without limitations. Be as greedy as you can. So, do you support capitalism or not? If you do, then where do you logically propose we find the money to make this happen?

Consider that there are roughly 31.5 million Americans that are between the ages of 18 and 24 currently. Taking the averages for annual tuition and fees of the average in-state public 4-year school ($9,400) and the average annual private nonprofit 4-year school ($32,400), that's $20,900 annually per student. If we really believe in sending every one of these people to college then that becomes $658 BILLION. Roughly. For one year. Of course this also doesn't account for any masters or doctoral programs. Supposedly, we can't feed everyone in this country, but we're going to propose spending $658 billion every year to send people to college? Could we possibly be any more callous toward human suffering? I for one am absolutely disgusted and appalled by the ignorant and heartless suggestion of free college for everyone in this country within the current capitalist confines.

According to recent statistics there are only 27 percent of college students that are currently working in a field that is related to their degree. It makes no sense to inundate the market with more college graduates. Perhaps, just maybe, this illogical push for more college students has to do with the fact that over the last 25 years colleges have become enormous money makers. Standards for acceptance and graduating have decreased in an effort to increase matriculation rates and keep those students for the full four years. Usually even longer. Having stringent eligibility standards and a record of weaning out all but the exceptional, sounds great when establishing the level of prestige for an institution, but it is terrible for the bottom line. And isn't that what college and everything else is all about today? Are we to believe that this seemingly needless push for more college graduates is not being influenced by universities that want to increase their profit margins? Student loans are guaranteed in a way that no other loan is. There is no defaulting out of it. Every student, whether they pay cash or credit is guaranteed income for the school. Now on top of that we're going to get the government to guarantee more payments and a drastic increase in the number of students.

While sending everyone to college is both grandiose and ideal it is simultaneously neither realistic nor pragmatic in the current capitalist economy. We support sending more people to college, regardless of an apparent lack of need to do so in the first place and with no intelligible plan to finance this reckless endeavor. How can one say it is unrealistically utopian to imagine a society practicing AISE and then make the argument that we should, for some unrealized reason, finance, in some as yet unknown manner, every person in this country going to college without consideration to their individual aptitude?

In AISE, education could be guaranteed through completion of high school as it is now. After that, every person who graduates with say a 2.5 GPA would be eligible to attend a university. Everyone should be required to take an aptitude test. Those who score highest would be given first choice and allowed to attend the more challenging universities. The aptitude scores would not dictate automatic exclusion or acceptance to any particular university or discipline, but they would serve as a means to determine an order of preference. Remember this is not a perfect system, but giving priority to those who score highest on an aptitude exam hardly seems arbitrary. It is no different than the current methodology except of course the fact that those with parents who have the means to make "donations" or pay the tuition in full, get preferential treatment now. At least this way, anyone who scored well could go to Yale, because there would be no economic dysfunction. Those who do not qualify or choose not to attend would begin an occupation instead. Going to college would no longer be a perk of the entitled and privileged, but an opportunity for all viable applicants to get an education. Minimum thresholds for grades should be established to suit specific universities and specific programs. Those who failed to meet these standards should either be transferred to a lower level university or program or start employment. In AISE there is no annual tuition bill that will only continuously grow.

As much as doctors get paid, don't most people still talk about the exorbitant student loan amounts that they become burdened with? This serves as a detractor for a number of people who might otherwise pursue such an occupation. Does it really make sense to intentionally establish hindrances to people who would otherwise be qualified to take on the training of a job that finds its focal point to be about caring for other members of society? I'm not talking about lowering the standards to make it easier for just anyone to become a doctor. Or talking about diminishing the esteem that accompanies the title, I'm just talking about pure financial hurdles. Even if one accepts that the doctor is in fact entitled to greater compensation for his/her social benefit, the rarity of their intelligence levels, or the prolonged education period, how does one logically justify the financial burden or possibly even blockade to making such a profession possible for anyone who qualifies? Wouldn't it behoove society to allow anyone who met the academic requirements to go to medical school and not allow financial burdens to impede them?

Currently in capitalism there is a vast amount of waste and inefficiency that AISE could quickly and seamlessly rectify. There are plenty of people right now who are coping with their current situations because they either lack the sufficient funds or appropriate insurance coverage to address the issue in question. We have people living in conditions that are affecting their health, like old, moldy central air ducts. Another example is people driving a vehicle that is not very safe or is leaking some fluid or another. People with chronic issues of pain or discomfort. Perhaps they have a mole or their vision is worsening and these issues should be addressed, but since they lack good enough insurance they are concerned by the cost that it will incur just to get these issues looked at, much less corrected. Let us not pretend that this is a rare and limited set of circumstances that I'm describing. Sadly, it is a rather common occurrence. So we have individuals who are polluting the environment more than is necessary and ignoring health issues which have the potential for being even more problematic and costly in the future. This is all because they do not have the sufficient funds to address these issues, which is due to capitalism intentionally making them "have nots".

We have the ability and resources to distribute the goods and services that society needs and desires, but we *choose* not to because of the manmade contrivances of our capitalist economic system. Right now we have empty recovery rooms and operating rooms, not because there is a lack of demand, but because you have a person with real chronic back pain that is just dealing with it, because they lack insurance or cash to pay for a necessary procedure. We currently have surpluses of goods and services that are not distributed because of capitalist economic technicalities. We have skilled and unskilled laborers who are willing and able to work, but are not because of the same technicalities. The truth is that by applying altruistic economics we have the ability to employ all these people in meaningful occupations that are productive. We also have the ability to dispense these services and goods to those that actually need them.

Instead of having to market differing quality levels of goods, we could do away with cheap, poorly constructed goods. Like the cheap plastic containers instead of high quality ones. Right now such choice is necessary because some people cannot afford a well-constructed container that would likely last them a lifetime. So we need to provide cheap options that will quickly break and get dumped into the trash, only to be replaced with new, affordable, cheap options. Many people can't afford $200 for a solid container, but they can manage to buy multiple $5 plastic containers over a few years. In AISE affordability is no longer a concern, so quality goods are the standard and thus there is less waste and garbage production. I'm not saying there will be only one option or style. I'm saying there is no need to produce cheap appliances that everyone knows will not last more than a couple years, and other items that are of poor quality and therefore really a waste of resources. The only reason they're made now is out of necessity to accommodate those without the means to buy these long lasting goods.

In AISE there is no need for all this marketing and advertising. It has been claimed that 100 million trees are destroyed every year in order to print the junk mail we all receive. In addition to this, practically every supermarket in this country prints up a new flyer every week to highlight the current sales and deals. Recycling or not, this is incredibly wasteful. All this waste is produced for the sole purpose of enticing people to purchase goods from one location over another. We tolerate unsightly billboards and energy wasting neon signs to tell us what we should be buying. None of this is necessary in AISE. Combining all the previous examples of waste consider how much more efficient we could be. Whether you believe in global warming or not, littering the landscape with worthless plastic junk and wasting paper every week is not an intelligent use of resources.

There may be fears by pessimists of AISE devolving into an abuse of power by the governing powers, where people will be arbitrarily denied services due to their minority status or in an effort to punish dissidents. Do we allow such things to occur now? So why is this the only imaginable future within AISE, which is still a republic? If anything, it would be a more virtuous version as special interest groups would lose their power of financial influence. We are currently willing to tolerate the inequality of one person being rich and thus being able to get whatever services they want at the highest quality. How can we not recognize that creating a system of triage for services based purely on need rather than financial wealth is not better? This does actually work with organ transplants and emergency rooms across the country, as well as other services. We have been so well conditioned into believing though, that price is the best and only way to determine who gets what goods and services. We have learned to accept this reprehensible and callous outlook that disregards need in favor of one's ability to pay more.

AISE is not about making copied drones out of everyone. It is about everyone feeling a sense of communal relationship in the wellbeing of others. Some people recoil at the Native American ideal that every woman in the tribe is mother to every baby in the tribe, because of a fear of loss of individuality. We currently rely on a system where we believe that the payment of $10/hour will be enough to make a relative stranger value our own children as much as their own family. As if that meager compensation will be enough to erase all the individual and profit driven motivators of capitalism. We expect the babysitter or daycare provider to put forth the same effort toward the nurturing and protecting of our baby/child as a family member would. Why are we shocked when a babysitter or daycare worker, motivated by nothing more than fiscal recompense, acts with disregard to the wellbeing of our kids? In the best interests of our kids, isn't it more logical for us to embrace an economic system that supports and nurtures feelings of altruistic responsibility toward everyone?

One of the purported fears of altruistic economics is how the godless, faceless, state/community will then assume all duties of education and will formulate the curriculum without any meaningful outsider input. What would one call public school? How does No Child Left Behind and Common Core not exactly exemplify this very concern? How are both of those initiatives not a godless, faceless, state/community formulating a curriculum without any meaningful outsider input? We recoil at the idea of the community taking ownership responsibility toward everyone, out of fear of loss of individual choice and family values. And yet that is exactly what we accept.

The following example is provided as nothing more than a glimpse at one possible methodology of implementing AISE. I offer it for the sole reason of proving that it is not my intent to propose a system without consideration of its practical application. Having said that, it is not the intent of this volume to become bogged down in details of specificity. It is not intended as a blueprint with the path to success laid out.

Suppose that someone decides to build a fancy tree fort in their backyard for their kids. Someone else sees it and likes it. They are both free to barter with what personal goods or services they each have, so that the first person is suitably enticed to build another tree fort for the second person. As long as each person continues to fulfill their pre-arranged obligations to society and that the construction of these units does not impede upon anyone else's rights or require the use of supplies and materials that are controlled by society and therefore would require public approval first. Now if you are pessimistically thinking that is too complex and convoluted, you clearly have never had to deal with zoning laws, building permits, and liability issues dealing with constructing a structure on someone else's property in our current system. Let us not have fanciful visions of simplicity for some imagined reality. Any cultured society requires a logical and respectful set of conditions to be met prior to undertaking this type of action.

If these tree forts were to become so popular that the original builder risked not having time enough to satisfy his social duties and/or the necessary supplies began to exceed the limits of personal holdings and thus required the use of materials under the purview of public control, then a request could be brought forth to make the construction of said tree forts a publicly available option. If it were democratically approved or approved through the proper channels of a republic, then the original builder would find herself reassigned from her previous social responsibility to this new occupation. Now we have a new product. It is made available for public consumption and a person is given the opportunity to create and hold an occupation that is creative and fulfilling. And thus we see one possible way of how goods and variety can be determined in AISE.

It is essential that we first, as a society, decide whether AISE is the correct choice. By that I mean, do we believe that it is plausible and does it satisfy the moral standards that we want to live by. Once that is decided, we can craft the means by which to make it a reality. One of the great problems we had with abolishing slavery in country was that the discussion was focused on *how* it could be abolished before it had been decided that it *should* be abolished. Instead of getting the majority of the population to understand that it was something that needed to be done, the discussion was almost immediately focused on how to make the abolition of slavery happen. Certainly there were attempts to do this and Harriet Beecher Stowe is the most famous example. But this was too little too late. Those who didn't believe that abolition was necessary certainly had no inclination to discuss how to make it happen. So by pushing the discussion for decades, of how to limit the expansion of slave states and minimize slave owner rights, more divisiveness was created. This is why the Civil War occurred and is also why it took so long for African Americans to truly get the equality they had been promised. On the other hand when you look at the American Revolution, they spent years winning people over and unifying the colonies under one singular opinion to revolt against royal tyranny. The Articles of Confederation aren't even written until more than a year after the war started and aren't ratified until 1781. The Constitution, written because the Articles of Confederation are deemed insufficient, isn't written until 1787.

The purpose of this chapter has been to offer a glimpse of how AISE can potentially operate and to demonstrate that it is not proposed without any consideration of its structure. As the history of this very country is proof of, the absence of a defined plan does not mean that the ideal is not worth pursuing. Thus it is the purpose of this volume to initiate a conversation to expose the lies and deceit of capitalism and to prove the ethical and humanitarian worth of AISE. Once we have become convinced that this is the right path for us to follow, then we can focus on formulating the plan. As our own history proves is possible.

Closing Thoughts

*You cannot escape the
responsibility of tomorrow by
evading it today.*

Abraham Lincoln

I hope that it is now evident to you how capitalism is designed to help the top one percent maintain their wealth and exploit the rest of us. That the principles extolled by Adam Smith and used as the frame work for our system are rife with bias toward the one percent. I hope you can see how the one percent manipulate supply, inflation, and promote conflict among the working segment. Do you recognize now how capitalism guarantees that there are always those who are less well off than others, as a necessity of its proper function? As a society we have accepted the belief that it is appropriate to consider a person's fiscal value before their worth as a human being. Virtually all religious and ethical standards that are commonly practiced, globally, reject this very mindset, yet we practice it in capitalism without hesitation.

The purpose of this first volume is to merely achieve the first phase that is required for cultural improvement, which is to create awareness and understanding. We must become cognizant of the moral depravity that we currently practice without remorse. Once we see the decrepitude in our own actions and value system that capitalism encourages, we can recognize that a better path is essential. It is for the sake of our spiritual wellbeing, if not for the cessation of the needless suffering we now listlessly accept. It is my sincere hope that this work will result in earnest dialogue and a search for a meaningful solution that legitimately merges morality into the economic fabric. It is possible to satisfy our physical needs, be productive, and be a vibrant progressive society without needing to utterly disregard the spiritual considerations.

Courage is not action in the absence of fear. Nor is courage action without thoughtful consideration. Those are called reckless abandon and there is nothing noble about that. Courage is the conviction to take action, motivated by moral beliefs, in the face of uncertainty and risk to one's own welfare. This is our chance to be courageous as a generation and as a society. This is our opportunity to build something bigger than ourselves. We don't need to read a history book or watch a blockbuster super hero movie, because we can do something brave and real right now. We may not ride off into the sunset, having defeated the great galactic evil and ensuring peace, life, and love forever. But we do have an opportunity to make an unrivaled positive impact on human wellbeing.

People will still die of cancer, monsters that prey on the innocent will still exist, and accidents will still happen. But those cancer patients will not die for want of proper care and the best possible medical resolution. Monsters will not be set free for cost cutting measures and the victims will not suffer for lack of suitable treatment and counseling. Accidents will not happen due to profit driven risk assessment and those left in their wake will not have to bear the financial burdens such events often create. You shower each day, even though you know you will just get dirty again. You spend money, even though you know you will just need to earn more. You perform countless actions, knowing that you will make mistakes and never achieve perfection. Yet none of these truths are enough to motivate you from giving up and doing nothing at all. Why should this be any different? Particularly when the potential good from such a decision is so enormous. The fact that bad things will continue to happen is a deplorable excuse for not preventing some future occurrences or easing the pain caused by bad things that have happened.

As individuals it is true that we are prisoners within the system of capitalism. One person or even a small group of people cannot hope to survive properly amidst such an overwhelming influence. But as individuals we can begin to talk and agree and create momentum. The task is daunting, but what if our predecessors had cowered at the task of setting the slaves free? What if they had withered in the face of royal oppression? We must rise above and do what we know to be right. More importantly we must know that we CAN. We know our current system is broken and unethical on so many levels. But it is not enough to just recognize and complain about inequality. We must actively seek a proper solution. The solution exists, we only need to put our minds to developing it.

Altruistically Inspired Societal Economics is possible as a functional system operating in conjunction with a republic. I have only begun to propose some of the ways that it is possible to operate. Certainly there is significantly more work that needs to be done, but there is nothing to indicate it is impossible. All that is required for Altruistically Inspired Societal Economics to work is our commitment to make it work. The only sociological achievements that are impossible are the ones that we believe are impossible. While there are other steps to make this a reality, at its core it really is just that simple. The purpose of this book is to stimulate conversation, with the anticipation that action will follow. I leave you with some ideas to ponder. If I have not completely convinced you that capitalism is a systematic means for the one percent to exploit us, I hope you can at least recognize its many shortcomings. Please consider the moral and ethical aspects that I presented. Then I would ask you to answer for yourself whether you truly believe that capitalism conforms to whatever spiritual or moral guidelines that you choose to follow. If your answer to yourself is no, then please contemplate why you continue to support capitalism.

I would like to thank you for taking the time to read this book and sincerely hope that I have moved you, at least to some degree. I would like to pose one last thought for consideration. A question worthy of "A Great Society". Do you believe that Altruistically Inspired Societal Economics is possible? Now I have never asserted, assumed, or implied that the perfect format for applying AISE exists yet. I openly acknowledge that it will take time and plenty of discussion to make it happen. So I ask you to reflect and consider: Do you believe that Altruistically Inspired Societal Economics is *possible?*

> *It always seems impossible until it's done.*
>
> Nelson Mandela

Notes

The College Board. (2015). Average Published Undergraduate Charges by
    Sector, 2015-16. Retrieved from:
    http://trends.collegeboard.org/college-pricing/figures-
    tables/average-published-undergraduate-charges-sector-2015-16

MarketingCharts staff. (April 28, 2015). So How Many Millennials Are There in
    the US, Anyway? (Updated). Marketing Charts. Retrieved from:
    http://www.marketingcharts.com/traditional/so-how-many-
    millennials-are-there-in-the-us-anyway-30401/

Brainyquote.com. Retrieved from:
    http://www.brainyquote.com/quotes/authors/a/abraham_lincoln.h
    tml

Plato. Reeve, C.D.C. reviser. Grube, G.M.A. translation. (November 15, 1992)
    The Republic 2nd edition. *Hackett Publishing Company, Inc.*
    Indianapolis, IN.

Plumer, Brad. (May 20, 2013). Only 27 Percent of College Grads Have a Job
    Related to Their Major.
    The Washington Post. Retrieved from:
    https://www.washingtonpost.com/news/wonk/wp/2013/05/20/onl
    y-27-percent-of-college-grads-have-a-job-   related-to-their-
    major/

Aristotle. Thomson, J.A.K. translator. (March 30, 2004). The Nicomachean
    Ethics New Ed edition. *Penguin Classics*. NYC, NY.

Kurt, Daniel. (Updated February 24, 2016). Are You in the Top One Percent of
    the World? *Investopedia*. Retrieved from:
    http://www.investopedia.com/articles/personal-
    finance/050615/are-you-top-one-percent-world.asp

Price, B.B. and Ambirajan, S. (1997). Ancient Economic Thought. *Routledge*.
    London, G.B. Retrieved from:
    http://www.law.yale.edu/documents/pdf/cbl/Khanna_Ancient_Indi
    a_informal.pdf

Gongloff, Mark. (Updated Sep 16, 2014). 45 Million Americans Still Stuck
    Below Poverty Line: Census*The Huffington Post*. Retrieved from:
    http://www.huffingtonpost.com/2014/09/16/poverty-household-
    income_n_5828974.html

Cline, Seth. (January 18, 2013). Meet the Five Poorest U.S. Senators. *U.S. News & World Report*. Retrieved from: http://www.usnews.com/news/articles/2013/01/18/the-five-poorest-us-senators

Frumin, Aliyah. (Updated September 13, 2013). How Much Does it Cost to Win a Seat in Congress? If You Have to Ask... *MSNBC*. Retrieved from: http://www.msnbc.com/hardball/how-much-does-it-cost-win-seat-congre

Frohlich, Thomas C., Sauter, Michael B., and Stebbins, Sam. (August 26, 2015). The Net Worth of Presidential Candidates. *USA Today*. Retrieved from: http://www.usatoday.com/story/news/politics/elections/2015/08/26/24-7-wall-st-net-worth-presidential-candidates/32409491/

Porretto, John and Charlton, Angela. (2008). Big Oil's Most Profitable Quarter Ever: $51.5 Billion. *ABC News*. Retrieved from: http://abcnews.go.com/Business/story?id=5503955

Food Bank Network. (2015). Feeding America 2015. Retrieved from: http://www.feedingamerica.org/about-us/how-we-work/food-bank-network/

National Cancer Institute. (2015). Surveillance, Epidemiology, and End Results Program. SEER Cancer Statistics Review. http://seer.cancer.gov/statfacts/html/all.html

Sherry Glied, Sherry PhD, Associate Professor of Public Health, Columbia University. LPB. Retrieved from: http://www.pbs.org/healthcarecrisis/uninsured.html

Gebleoff, Robert and Dewan, Shaila. (January 17, 2012). Measuring the Top 1% by Wealth, Not Income. *New York Times*. Retrieved from: http://economix.blogs.nytimes.com/2012/01/17/measuring-the-top-1-by-wealth-not-income/?_r=0

Delafuente, Charles. (February 11, 2013). Borrowing From the Future. *New York Times*. Retrieved from: http://www.nytimes.com/2013/02/12/business/early-withdrawals-plague-retirement-accounts-study-says.html?_r=0

Van Dyke, Aly. (July 14, 2013). Records Show 17 Nonprofit Executives Receive Six-Figure Salaries. *Cjonline.com*. Retrieved from: http://cjonline.com/news/2013-07-14/records-show-17-nonprofit-executives-receive-six-figure-salaries

Kaplan, Larry. (October 14, 2013). CNN Is Shocked: Some Big Nonprofit CEOs Make over $1 Million. *CNN Money*. Retrieved from: https://nonprofitquarterly.org/2013/10/14/cnn-is-shocked-some-big-nonprofit-ceos-make-over-1-million/

The KJV Study Bible. (2011) King James Version. *Barbour Publishing Inc*. Uhrichsville, OH.

Marx, Karl and Engels, Friedrich. (February 21, 1848). The Communist Manifesto. *SoHo Books*. USA.

More, Thomas. (2001) Utopia. *Yale University Press*. New Haven, CT.

Mandela, Nelson. (February 3, 2005). The Full Text of Nelson Mandela's Speech in London's Trafalgar Square. *BBC News*. Retrieved from: http://news.bbc.co.uk/2/hi/uk_news/politics/4232603.stm

Quranic Arabic Corpus. (2009-2011). Arberry Translation. *Kais Dukes*. Retrieved from: http://corpus.quran.com/translation.jsp?chapter=5&verse=8

Blodget, Henry. (March 23, 2012). There Are Now More Americans In Jail Than There Were In Stalin's Gulag Archipelago. *Business Insider*. Retrieved from: http://www.businessinsider.com/how-many-americans-in-jail-2012-3

Raphael, Steven and Stoll, Michael A. (2008). Why Are So Many Americans in Prison? *Russell Sage Foundation*. New York. Retrieved from: https://www.law.berkeley.edu/img/why_are_so_many_americans_in_prison%281%29.pdf

DiBlasio, Natalie. (August 17, 2014). Hunger in America: 1 in 7 rely on food banks. *USA Today*. Retrieved from: http://www.usatoday.com/story/news/nation/2014/08/17/hunger-study-food/14195585/

Forbes Quotes (2015). Thoughts On The Business Of Life. *Forbes.com LLC*. Retrieved from: http://www.forbes.com/quotes/6686/

Building a Better America survey, Norton and Ariely (2010). *Tampa Bay Times*. Retrieved from: http://www.tampabay.com/specials/2010/graphics/wealth-graphics/

Pixabay.com Retrieved from: https://pixabay.com/en/social-media-faces-social-networks-550766/

Infoplease. *United States Unemployment Rates*. Retrieved from: http://www.infoplease.com/ipa/A0104719.html

United States Department of Labor. Bureau of Labor Statistics. *Household Data Annual Averages*. Retrieved from: http://www.bls.gov/cps/cpsaat01.htm

Yanke, Ryan (July 29, 2014). Lack of Poverty in Finland. *Borgen*. Retrieved from: http://www.borgenmagazine.com/lack-of-poverty-in-finland/

Ryland, Julie Ryland (January 1, 2014).Norwegians' poverty falls while rate increases in the EU. *The Norway Post*. Retrieved from: http://www.norwaypost.no/index.php/news/latest-news/29385-norwegians-poverty-declines-while-the-rate-increases-across-europe

41pounds.org. Retrieved from: https://www.41pounds.org/impact/

O'Rourke, Ciara. (March 16, 2009). Reducing the Junk Mail Footprint. *The New York Times*. Retrieved from: https://www.catalogchoice.org/environmental-facts

Hartman, Eviana. (January 20, 2008). How to Junk Junk Mail and Other Paper Clutter. *The Washington Post*. Retrieved from: http://www.washingtonpost.com/wp-dyn/content/article/2008/01/17/AR2008011701793.html

Mahapatra, Lisa. (June 10, 2013). Worst Charities: The "Non Profits" That Spend Most Of Their Money On Fundraising. *IBTimes*. Retrieved from: http://www.ibtimes.com/worst-charities-non-profits-spend-most-their-money-fundraising-1298829

Sullivan, Patrick. (August 18, 2012). Charity Overhead Should Be 23 Percent, But Most Spend Much More: Report. *Huffington Post*. Retrieved from: http://www.huffingtonpost.com/2012/08/18/charity-overhead-23-percent_n_1803027.html

Mittendorf, Brian. (April 23, 2013). Do Nonprofits Really Limit Advertising Because of Pressure to Cut Overhead? *Nonprofit Quarterly*. Retrieved from: https://nonprofitquarterly.org/2013/04/23/do-nonprofits-really-limit-advertising-because-of-pressure-to-cut-overhead/

Howard, Robert E. Howard, Milius, John, Stone, Oliver, and Summer, Edward. (May 14, 1982). Conan the Barbarian. *Universal Pictures (presents) Dino De Laurentiis Company.*

Handwerk, Brian. (October 8, 2013). Why Some Animals Mate Themselves to Death. *National Geographic*. Retrieved from: http://news.nationalgeographic.com/news/2013/10/131007-marsupials-mammals-sex-mating-science-animals/

The BBC. (2016) Retrieved from:http://www.bbc.co.uk/nature/adaptations/Semelparity_and_it eroparity